artful stories

Rochelle Brock and Richard Greggory Johnson III
Executive Editors

Visual Arts and Music
Mary Weems, Series Editor

Vol. 22

The Black Studies and Critical Thinking series
is part of the Peter Lang Education list.
Every volume is peer reviewed and meets
the highest quality standards for content and production.

PETER LANG
New York • Washington, D.C./Baltimore • Bern
Frankfurt • Berlin • Brussels • Vienna • Oxford

Joanne Kilgour Dowdy

artful stories

The Teacher, the Student, and the Muse

To: Christa
all the best, all the days!
Joanne Dowdy
2012

PETER LANG
New York • Washington, D.C./Baltimore • Bern
Frankfurt • Berlin • Brussels • Vienna • Oxford

Library of Congress Cataloging-in-Publication Data

Dowdy, Joanne Kilgour.
Artful stories: the teacher, the student, and the muse / Joanne Kilgour Dowdy.
p. cm. — (Black studies and critical thinking; v. 22)
Includes bibliographical references and index.
1. Blacks in the performing arts—United States.
2. Performing arts—Study and teaching—United States.
3. Caribbean Americans—Interviews. 4. Educators—United States—Interviews.
5. Performing artists—United States—Interviews. I. Title.
PN1590.B53D69   792.092'396972983—dc23   2011046861
ISBN 978-1-4331-1408-3 (hardcover)
ISBN 978-1-4331-1407-6 (paperback)
ISBN 978-1-4539-0524-1 (e-book)
ISSN 1947-5985

Bibliographic information published by **Die Deutsche Nationalbibliothek**.
Die Deutsche Nationalbibliothek lists this publication in the "Deutsche
Nationalbibliografie"; detailed bibliographic data is available
on the Internet at http://dnb.d-nb.de/.

For
All the Men
Who
Labor on
in
Silence.

Thank You.

Contents

Editor's Preface

Mary Weems

I met Joanne approximately eight years ago through a playwright friend. There was something in the vibe between us that felt like *home*, as if I'd known her all of my life even though we're from two different parts of the world. Our first conversation was like every one we've had since then, filled with rapid talk about the arts, the amazing possibility each day is, and the importance of living in the moment with love, compassion, grace, and peace. Joanne is the first qualitative researcher I've met whose research agenda is centered in the importance of focusing on what's working in her field. As she shared with me: *"There are enough people* [including me] *focusing on problems, I don't want to live in that place."*

Reading William Kist's introduction to this book reminded me of my first visit to Joanne's office. I was struck by the beautiful cloth draped in the doorway, the personal artifacts that made the space feel like a Black person's living room and all of the examples of student work that decorated the walls like mini-lessons in what it means to understand the many ways literacy operates when given a chance to spread its wings in directions which move beyond letters on a page.

I complimented Joanne on the way she'd managed to carve out a space for art and the heart in an academy where décor typically means blank beige walls, dull carpeting, file cabinets, cluttered desks, and an occasional piece of too expensive 'art' which typically doesn't make me feel or think anything. I remembered her office when I set up my own a few years later and created my space following her lead.

As a poet, playwright, artist-scholar, imagination-intellect theorist (See Weems, 2003) and lover of words, I'd never thought much about multiple literacies until I met Joanne. Now, I think about them often and provide space in each education class I teach for a variety of ways to explore literacy within the context of course goals and assignments including music, dance, visual art and multi-media creations. When I was selected by Peter Lang as one of ten series editors for the Black Studies in Critical Thinking series, I sent out the following call:

What's Going On: Black Studies and the Arts:

Historically, Black artists and scholars have used their work to investigate and articulate the heart of the global Black experience. We seek work that addresses innovative ways visual art, music, poetry, literature, dance, and other art forms critique, illuminate and/or bear witness to problems and solutions to critical issues in K–12 and postsecondary education. These issues include but are not limited to use of the arts as an integral part of the curriculum to critique or explore the achievement gap, to report on the consequences of No Child Left Behind, use of the arts in Teacher Education programs, and the experiences of Black artist-scholars in academia. We are interested in authors who are doing qualitative research using interpretive methods including auto/ethnography, ethnography, poetic inquiry, narrative, and ethnodrama as well as interview and focus groups. What's Going On welcomes work from all educational disciplines and will also consider collaborative book projects on the cutting edge of crucial issues facing Black people today.

The first book proposal I received was Joanne's. As an artist-scholar, my series is grounded in the theory that imagination-intellectual development through the arts should be the primary goal of education. One of the five components of imagination-intellectual development is the effect of the arts on social consciousness and ways the arts can be used to counter racism, speak truth to power, and to argue against all forms of social injustice. Understanding too that thanks to the Black Diaspora our people are scattered all over the world, I was immediately interested in a book which proposed an up-close and personal look at four Caribbean born artists living, teaching and working on the socially constructed margins of North America. These are Black men who have not forgotten their roots, who have acted as teachers and mentors to new generations of artists in lighting design and production, choreography, jazz music and dance.

Artful Stories: The Teacher, the Student, and the Muse invites the reader to take a journey with Joanne across the lives of Gerard, the lighting designer/production manager, Leo, the choreographer, Richard, the jazz musician, and Hugo, the dancer (all pseudonyms). They are Black men she interviewed periodically over a seven-year period, exploring their Caribbean origins, personal accomplishments as artists, their work with students as well as their challenges and disappointments as members of an internationally marginalized group.

As we got to know each other, Joanne and I discovered many connections beyond our race and gender, including the fact that our fathers were both athletes. Her book opens with the following lines:

> *I buried my father in 2004. It was six months after my sister's funeral. During the week after the rituals that accompany the choosing of a coffin, asking someone to deliver the sermon at the service, and choosing the right chapel for the "thanksgiving" ceremony, I made a decision to do a project in honor of my father and the men who peopled my life as an artist.*

Here Joanne honors her father and accomplished Black men everywhere, with and without formal degrees. I'm honored to begin my series with this book. Enjoy the journey.

Mary E. Weems
Assistant Professor
John Carroll University
University Hts., Ohio

Foreword by William Kist

Associate Professor
Kent State University
Kent, Ohio

Joanne Kilgour Dowdy is my next-door neighbor within our college at Kent State University. Occasionally, we are in our building at the same time and I get a chance to pop into her office. It is like traveling back to another time in my life when I was a more active musician and video director. Many professors' offices seem oddly conformist, with the generic messy stacks of old handouts, the unread books leaning precipitously off the dusty wooden shelves and the faded *New Yorker* cartoons stuck up somewhere. In contrast, Joanne's office is a work of art itself. Filled with color and light and atypical furniture, the space is crammed with work from various artists and former students. Her office is an oasis in what's referred to as the "Ivory Tower."

I thought of Joanne's office as I read this book. Like her office space, this book is filled with light and drama and story. I know that I must eventually return to my office filled with mounting "data" that has to be assessed for the latest round of accreditation "self-study," but as I read these chapters, I find myself questioning why I have to go back to that.

The irony of this tension is that we educators have a greater need for dialogue with artists than ever before. In a time when the very act of "reading" involves interaction with not only print, but visual images (both moving and still), music, graphic design, and even advertising, it would seem that now, more than at any time in our long history of formal education, we need to bring artists into the mainstream of teaching and learning. For our students' very survival in this hyper-linked world, we must equip them with the crafts and, perhaps even, the aptitudes and attitudes, of the artists profiled in this book. And, yet, in many of our schools in North America, the arts are still referred to as "specials."

This distancing of the arts from the "regular" classroom has a long history. Many have called for a greater integration of the arts even before the Internet has prodded us in that direction. As early as 1934, John Dewey was lamenting that we had lost the closeness to the arts that people of an earlier time had (Dewey, 1934/1980). At that time, Dewey was complaining about the formal institutionalization of the arts. One wonders if Dewey might actually be relieved about the way the new media have brought theater, film, dance, and music into our daily lives. In an age when a click of the mouse can bring us to either a YouTube clip of Toscanini conducting the NBC Orchestra or to a clip of a kitten playing the piano, it's clear we very much need an integra-tion of an aesthetic sense and an informed discussion of the arts in our classrooms, an interweaving of the true meaning of symbolic represen-tation and the affordances of many kinds of symbol systems into our everyday school lives.

When I started to research the new literacies movement, I was capti-vated by Vera John-Steiner's phrase "cognitive pluralism" (John-Steiner, 1997). At that time, Eliot Eisner was also pointing out the impact of the arts on cognition (1994, 1997), and Howard Gardner was pointing out that we are all a mix of multiple intelligences (1983, 1993). These were writers who believed, apart from the existence of any piece of hardware or software, that we have been cheating our students by privileging print-based literacies. While there is certainly no doubt that all humans need to have the capability to read print, the fact that most, if not all, of the school day is dominated by print and mathematical literacies has disenfranchised a whole host of students who see the world in different ways and are most apt to express themselves in non-print media.

As the new media began to proliferate in the 1990s, there were different names for what I tend to call "new literacies." There have also been multiple frameworks for studying these new literacies, with most of them focusing on the social contexts for their uses. The focus on the social practices and events associated with literacy has formed the core of what have become known as the New Literacy Studies which Lankshear and Knobel (2003) define as referring to "a specific socio-cultural approach to understanding and researching literacy" (p. 16). If we are to look at literacy as inextricably linked to social context, then linked to that focus may be criticism of the power structure in that social context, as well as its prevailing discourses (Fairclough, 1989, 1995). As Rogers (2002) defined this perspective, "Critical literacy concerns itself with disrupting dominant social practices through resistant reading and writing of texts" (p. 773).

Fortunately, there also continue to be some researchers who look at new literacies through an arts lens, whether it's through examining classrooms in which a knowledge of aesthetics is taught (Vasudevan, 2010; Dickson and Costigan, 2011) or in which there is a focus on one artistic element, such as visual literacy (Serafini, 2011; Seglem and Witte, 2009) or theatre (Vasinda and McLeod, 2011) or film (Hodges, 2010). There have also been studies that have looked at multiple forms of representation according to the semiotics tradition (Iddings, McCafferty, and Teixeira da Silva, 2011; Wilson, 2011). Looking at these new media from an arts perspective continues to be rare, however, and that's what makes this book so refreshingly "retro."

The four artists' journeys depicted in this book exemplify the classic role artists have played as "teacher" to their students since the beginning of human expression, since before there was a word for "apprentice." As you will see, Gerard, the lighting designer/production manager, Leo, the choreographer, Richard, the jazz musician, and Hugo, the dancer, often seem as excited, if not more excited, about the work of their students as they are about their own work.

And work it is. The "blood, sweat and tears" of the teachers and students are evident in this book—this is not playtime. That's yet another irony of the predominant view of the arts as "specials." Anyone who has ever rehearsed to be in a play or spent hundreds of hours creating a painting knows how much work it is—work on a much more engaged, and meaningful level than any rote formulaic worksheet or paper/pencil test could be. When one practices for five hours a day to master an intricate piece of choreography, or sweats through a couple of shirts laboring over the composing of just the right 500 words, one has a right to say what "work" is. The men in this book, and their students, know what that work is.

I've always been struck by how kids who work in the arts are transformed and very quickly take on a maturity and a sense of teamwork that I believe to be quite healthy. This is not to say that they are not playful or that they don't enjoy being kids while they are being creative. But our society tends to marginalize kids and protect them to such a degree that it is probably only in the arts and athletics (that have, unfortunately, become so commercialized) that kids have a chance to really think and act as full-fledged human beings. In other facets of kids' lives, we tend to infantilize them. This is even though the idea of "childhood" and "adolescence" are actually fairly recent social constructions (Mintz, 2007; Savage, 2007). Our society has (for the most part) eradicated child labor and, over the last century, young people have enjoyed a prolonged "adolescence" that would not be recognizable to people of earlier centuries. Schools have served a vital protective role as they have stood over the children "in loco parentis," in place of the parents who are elsewhere during the school day. Of course, we all know that, even in the midst of this sheltering, we still have a too-high rate of poverty amongst our young people, with a substantial number of our youth describing themselves as "heavy drinkers" and sexually active (ChildStats.gov, 2008). Just how "safe" are kids in this new media age in which some estimates suggest that 8–18 year olds spend an average of 7.5 hours per day using entertainment media with using social networking sites as the most popular computer activity in this age group (Kaiser Family Foundation, 2010). The artists portrayed in this book provide venues for kids to give expression to the tensions and very real challenges that exist in their lives. What better way than through the arts to provide this outlet?

And, significantly, the four artists portrayed in these pages have been doing much of this work far from home. This was an element of the book that fascinated me, as someone who has never lived far from his hometown. I felt jealous, in a way, of these artists. But I suppose their journeys may be seen metaphorically. And that is the real point of education, isn't it? To go places we haven't gone before. The arts give us this ability to leave our essential spaces even if we don't ever physically go far. As Hugo says, "We have to write our plays, brother, because we are human beings like anybody else" (p. 20). I suppose it is this underlying humanity that fascinated me about this book, even though I am a white man who still lives close to his birthplace.

After all, even though my office is much less interesting than Joanne's, she and I have come to teaching and learning from a similar perspective in that we are both artists at heart. And what a benefit this has been to us as teachers! As Joanne points out in her opening chapter, "Dance, drama, music, and theater arts like lighting design, can alleviate some of the miscommunication within multi-ethnic classrooms" (p. 7). So many times I saw this in my own classroom. I remember that I was only a second-year English teacher when I stumbled across an abandoned piano in my school. I asked my principal if I could have it, even though I didn't teach music. To his credit (I do want to credit him by name—Raoul Bolock), he said yes, even though it meant he had to get piano movers to move it from a different floor. To this day, when I run into former students, they remember that I would sometimes play the piano for them, and often for no reason at all.

I have also long been interested in filmmaking and used early versions of the camcorder to allow students to create film adaptations of the classics. I still hear from a group of young black men who remember the epic video version of "The Knight's Tale" from "The Canterbury Tales." This early work in classroom video became my entrée into studying new literacies, as the Internet was being born just as I transitioned into higher education. My main goal in studying new literacies in the classroom has not come from my interest in gadgetry, but in the freeing quality, the breathing quality, that the arts brought to my classroom and the others I've studied. I don't get excited about the features of iCloud, for example, but in the potential new media bring for a greater range of human expression. The greatest benefit of the hardware and software has been the resulting venue for conversation about creativity and human expression via the arts that I did not have when I started teaching.

But I have a feeling that Joanne and I and the men profiled in this book would "do" the arts every day that we could, regardless of its applications to "new literacies," just because the arts are so inseparable from our essential selves. As Joanne says in her opening chapter, "There are phrases and paragraphs from the interviews carried out since 2004 that stay in my mind" (p. 19). I predict the stories in this book will stay in your mind, as well, as they have in mine. Now, if you'll excuse me, I have to practice my piano.

References

ChildStats.gov (2008). *American's children in brief: Key national indicators of well being, 2008.* Retrieved November 15, 2008, from: http://www.childstats.gov/americas-children/index.asp

Dewey, J. (1934/1980). *Art as experience.* New York: Perigee Books.

Dickson, R., and Costigan, A. (Jan. 2011). Emerging practice for new teachers: Creating possibilities for "aesthetic" readings. *English Education, 43*(2), 145–170.

Eisner, E. (1997). Cognition and representation: A way to pursue the American dream? *Phi Delta Kappan, 78,* 349–353.

Eisner, E. (1994) *Cognition and curriculum reconsidered* (2nd ed.). New York: Teachers College Press.

Fairclough, N. (1995). *Critical discourse analysis: The critical study of language.* New York: Longman.

Fairclough, N. (1989). *Language and power.* London: Longman.

Gardner, H. (1993). *Multiple intelligences: The theory into practice.* New York: Basic Books.

Gardner, H. (1983). *Frames of mind: The theory of multiple intelligences.* New York: Basic Books.

Hodges, A.L. (2010). A critical close-up: Three films and their lessons in critical literacy. *English Journal, 99*(3), 70–75.

Iddings, A.C.D., McCafferty, S.G., & Teixeira da Silva, M.L. (2011). Conscientizacao through graffiti literacies in the streets of a Sao Paulo neighborhood: An ecosocial semiotic perspective. *Reading Research Quarterly, 46*(1), 5–21.

John-Steiner, V. (1997). *Notebooks of the mind: Explorations of thinking (Rev. ed.).* New York: Oxford University Press.

Kaiser Family Foundation. (2010). *Generation M²: Media in the lives of 8- to 18-year olds.* Retrieved, from http://www.kff.org/entmedia/upload/8010.pdf

Lankshear, C., & Knobel, M. (2003). *New literacies: Changing knowledge and classroom learning.* Buckingham. UK: Open University Press.

Mintz, S. (2004). *Huck's raft: A history of American childhood.* Cambridge, MA: The Belknap Press of Havard University Press.

Rogers, R. (2002). "That's what you're here for, you're suppose to tell us": Teaching and learning critical literacy. *Journal of Adolescent & Adult Literacy, 45,* 772–787.

Savage, J. (2007). *Teenage: The creation of youth culture.* New York: Viking.

Seglem, R., & Witte, S. (2009). You gotta see it to believe it: Teaching visual literacy in the English classroom. *Journal of Adolescent & Adult Literacy, 53*(3), 216–226.

Serafini, F. (2011). Expanding perspectives for comprehending visual images in multi-modal texts. *Journal of Adolescent & Adult Literacy, 54,* 342–350.

Vasinda, S., & McLeod, J. (2011). Extending readers theatre: A powerful and purposeful match with podcasting. *The Reading Teacher, 64,* 486–497.

Vasudevan, L. (2010). Literacies in a participatory, multimodal world: The arts and aesthetics of web 2.0. *Language Arts, 88*(1), 43–50.

Wilson, A.A. (2011). A social semiotics framework for conceptualizing content area literacies. *Journal of Adolescent & Adult Literacy, 54,* 435–444.

Preface

I buried my father in 2004. It was six months after my sister's funeral. During the week after the rituals that accompany the choosing of a coffin, asking someone to deliver the sermon at the service, and choosing the right chapel for the "thanksgiving" ceremony, I made a decision to do a project in honor of my father and the men who peopled my life as an artist. It worked out that I had a meeting with one of the male artists who appears in a chapter of this book. Hugo, as I decided to call this artist when I described him and his career in theater, was the first person who inspired me to do the research on four male, Trinidadian artists who I had grown up working with on stage and television, or met later in my performing career.

The four Black men who agreed to be interviewed over more than three years represent dance, drama, music, and lighting design. They are men who are well known in their fields and in the professional lives in their home island as well as in the USA and Canada. I wanted to document their evolution from the small theaters where they began their careers, to the wider world of performance arts that they participate in at this mature stage of their lives.

More importantly, I wanted to document the lives of men whom I consider significant to the development of the theater tradition in their home country. In my mind I was seeking out "exemplary" teachers. This criteria would be met if the participant had a successful career in the arts and was now teaching in higher education. Each participant also had to be Black, male, and from the same Caribbean island. This criteria was created because my father was an Olympic athlete, and it was not until very late in his life that he was sought out by journalists and other academicians for his history as a young competitor who grew up to participate in an international event when he was in his 20s. Knowing my father's struggle with what he considered the "scant courtesy" with which his government and peers treated him on his return from the Helsinki Olympics in 1952 has given me a sensitivity to the kinds of obstacles that "firsts" in any profession had to endure in order to make their name at home and abroad. While I have always felt that I am too close to my father's story to "get it right" for the sake of posterity, and a book deal, I do believe that I can document the story of similar cases that represent a struggle to "make a way out of no way."

When I left my home almost 30 years ago, my father cautioned me not to return to the country if I wanted to live a fulfilling professional life. He had the experience of coming home to a place that he believed was not as advanced in athletics as his committed life as a sportsman demanded. I, being "daddy's girl," have kept his voice alive in me over these three decades. In the face of many challenges as a Black, female, immigrant professional, I have remained outside my home country and developed my life as an academician. This experience has led me to make connections with other immigrants from my country who have chosen to stay outside their nation, to remain in the metropolis as we refer to our various exiles of choice, so that we can further our careers and "see our way" as our beloved Andre Tanker of Trinidad has sung.

What have the men in this book learned about being outside their homelands over their sojourn of decades abroad? Is it different than what I have gleaned in my determined progress up the educational ladder? In some ways my journey is reflected in the way that my determination to succeed informed my choices as an artist. Sometimes the doggedness to reach the top of your profession actually cuts off options that may have been more lucrative. Always, it seems, the family of an artist has to understand that unremitting longing to create a new work. There is always someone in the artist's life who is made to witness the effort this creator makes to contribute a new way of delivering an idea that is offered in the productions of others. There is a price to pay for artistic success and so the theme of "no free lunch" underlies the stories in these men's lives.

Also, there is the fact of the loneliness of the pursuit of the ideal, whatever it may look like to an individual creator. This dogged pursuit of the "perfect" dance move, lighting effect, or musical arrangement may seem like nonsense to the casual observer. It may test the limits of the patience of those who want to believe in the individual artist's integrity and talent. In many cases, "time is longer than twine" as my grandmother would say, and the artist runs afoul of those who want results, profits, quality time with the family or lovers. What to do? My dear aunt who is 84 years old would say, "They put you so," and shrug her shoulders. She knows that God has some preordained plan for each of us. We cannot escape our destiny and so it is best to make peace with it. And, of course, common sense dictates that we should pray for those who people the lives of artists. It takes a lot of patience to work and live with those people who believe that their life in the arts is a calling, not a job.

Chapter One

The Context of the Artists' Lives

If I could imagine the shaping of Fate,
I would think of blackmen
Handling the sun.

~Raymond Patterson

Afro Caribbeans Abroad

In 2009, Keane, Tappen, Williams, and Rosselli reported that 1.5 million immigrants from the Caribbean were living in the USA, and that the number was growing. This group of citizens is sometimes described as a "model minority" (Glazer & Moynihan, 1964; Sowell, 1978). In consideration of some of the obstacles that this population has to face and overcome in their lives in the USA, Bryce-Laporte (1972) discussed the challenges of xenophobia and racism as mitigating factors in their transition from a majority culture in their original homes to the minority culture of the metropolis. Some writers describe the Afro-Caribbean's "dual status" as both Black and "immigrant" (Kalmijn, 1996) and suggest that this causes conflicts within the Black American community and the global immigrant community within which the Afro Caribbeans may find themselves once they move onto the mainland. The literature that looks at the Afro Caribbean reactions to their new political place as minority citizens also raises questions about their perception of their ethnic identity (Waters, 1991), their political status (Kasinitz, 1992), and their role in labor markets (Model, 1991).

In the face of discrimination, confrontation over the difference in ethnic identity in comparison to the mainstream White American population, and the challenge of internalization of racist notions of inferiority, Afro-Caribbean immigrants are reported to make choices that are healthier for them (Read, Emerson, & Tarlov, 2005). Living within communities that are highly populated by immigrants from their native country and keeping in touch with family and support groups from their original homes reinforces their sense of psychological well-being (Deaux, 2006), and enhances their chances of making positive choices that sustain healthy lifestyles. Even within the challenges of the multiethnic Black community during the Harlem Renaissance (Watkins-Owen, 1996), noted authors such as Claude McKay, Eric Walrond, Rudolph Fisher, and Wallace Thurman had experiences and made observations of cultural adaptation that supported their representations of the diversity of race that Black America represented to immigrants.

Afro Caribbean Performing Artists

A slew of names of Caribbean performing artists come to mind when calling up the parade of successes that have graced the professional stage in the USA and beyond. Harry Belafonte, The Mighty Sparrow, Lord Kitchener, Heather Headley, Geoffrey Holder, Bob Marley, Sheryl Lee Ralph, Sidney Poitier, Madge St. Clair, and Lorraine Toussaint are just a few of the notables who have become international celebrities while plying their trade in the public domain.

Less recognizable names, though no less celebrated in their respective fields, are the performers like Natalie Rogers-Cropper who was the principal dancer for the Garth Fagan Dance Company and twice a winner of Broadway's most prestigious award: The Bessie. Also, there is

Kelvin Rotardier who performed with the Alvin Ailey Dance Company from its inception and is still associated with the present company. The Martha Graham Dance Company has employed two men from Trinidad over its long history, one of whom is Roger Shim. He has gone on to lead his own dance company. In the drama field, Michael Rogers has continued to represent the Caribbean aesthetic on stage and in film since his graduation from the Yale drama school. Veterans of jazz music would recognize the names of Monty Alexander, and Jon Lucien, but they would be hard pressed to describe the Caribbean roots of Sonny Rollins who won a 2010 Presidential Award from President Barack Obama.

The Caribbean artist works within and on the margins of the professional theater world in the USA and Canada. Unseen to all but the most discerning eye, and unheralded except to those who value history and the impact of Pan-Africanism across the world, the artists who contribute to the rich soil of creativity in the world of the performing arts can be found and counted among the most successful in their respective fields of activity.

Multiliteracies

Beach and Myers (2001) suggested that we ask students to look into the way that symbols, that is, words, actions, and pictures, help create systems that mediate our world as we experience it. Kist (2002) observed that the use of non-print-based media supported student development in fluency that was not otherwise observed in more traditional classrooms. The brain, Jacobs (2007) asserted, is helped to process information when it is presented in a variety of ways, and classrooms that encourage multiple ways of expressing meaning are successful sites where students find student-centered instruction appealing and educational.

Recognized as a world view that uses an aesthetic approach to reading the world (Rosenblatt, 1978), many teachers create arts based classrooms where students develop communication skills beyond reading, writing, speaking, listening, and signing, and include the visual, kinaesthetic, and aural arts to facilitate success within and beyond the classroom (Doig & Sargent, 1996; Harste, 1994; Reiff, 1992).

The classrooms in which students and teachers from diverse backgrounds interact are, essentially, intercultural spaces (Stewart & Bennett, 1972). Using cultural symbols that these participants are familiar with, and value (Dodd, 1992; Porter & Samovar, 1994; Samovar & Porter, 1999; Samovar, Porter, & Jain, 1981), can create opportunities for all participants to learn and expand their understanding of beliefs, attitudes, language, nonverbal communication, norms, rules, activities, time orientation, spatial relations, worldview, social organization, history, personality, material culture, and art (Stephan & Stephan, 1996). As teachers learn to include cultural signs, especially those that relate to a person's identity, the relationships between culture, race, ethnicity, and identity, they encourage their students to manipulate and appreciate arts based techniques in the classroom (Jones, 1990; Tatum, 1997).

Dance, drama, music, and theater arts, such as lighting design, can alleviate some of the miscommunication within multi-ethnic classrooms. Language minority groups can be greatly assisted in experiencing successful dialogue with their majority classmates with the help of arts based teaching techniques that do not rely on print communication. Since cross-cultural communication challenges usually stem from a need to have shared meaning (Senge, Kleiner, Roberts, Ross, & Smith, 1994), demanding a collective sense of what is important and why, the arts based inspired classroom is an ideal laboratory to test and perfect communication techniques that promote multiple forms of communication.

According to Kress, Jewitt, Ogborn, and Tsatsarelis (2001), a multimodal perspective of the classroom sees language appearing as speech or writing, visual expressions, or action, to make meaning. Informed by the social semiotics research of Halliday (1985), Jewitt et al. (2001) believed that learning is a dynamic process that is social by nature. The need to communicate among persons leads to the use of signs such as speech, writing, image, gesture, and three-dimensional models, among other forms of expression. Other writers support the reading and making of signs such as music (Van Leeuwen, 1999), action (Kress & Van Leeuwen, 1996; Martinec, 1996), as well as the use of visual communication (O'Toole, 1994).

My Background

I believe that I am obligated to give this description to validate any possible bias my personal background as a Black, female, artist, teacher, and immigrant may have contributed to this study. Because I have known these artists in a professional capacity as long as 35 years in one case, and as little as 7 years in another case, I bring a lot of background information on the milieu in which the artists operate to the study at hand.

In other publications I have described the fact that I come from a majority experience as an Afro-Caribbean (Delpit & Dowdy, 2002; Dowdy, 2008). I have also explained the fact that my native country is a Black republic and that my parents finished high school. Both parents worked in the civil service. My mother once worked in the Prime Minister's office as a secretary and my father was employed as a manager on the port of the capital of the country. Further, I completed high school in Trinidad and began my career as a teacher in middle and high school, and also held jobs as an actress and dancer on stage and in television productions (Dowdy & Golden, 2011).

On my journey as an acting student through the Juilliard School in New York, teaching at a middle school in Harlem, working in Wilmington, North Carolina, or doing research as the assistant director of the Center for the Study of Adult Literacy in Atlanta, Georgia, I found that I had to be educated to understand the ways of being a Black, literate female in the USA. Having documented the experiences of Black people, especially those who are educated in the formal sense, and particularly Black women, has opened my eyes to some of the challenges and triumphs that are strewn on the path to success in predominantly White institutions (Dowdy, 2003, 2005, 2008; Dowdy & Wynne, 2005; Dowdy & Golden, 2011).

Being Black, female, a teacher, and an artist gives me a high level of credibility among others with similar backgrounds in education, the performing arts, or the immigrant experience. My affinity with other educated immigrant men and women who find themselves in the higher education environment has opened doors for me to collect first-person accounts from fellow artists for this research project. I appear in this project as a participant-observer who mines the information that I gained as early as my teens to prompt and encourage my four male participants to share their stories from the perspective of our shared backgrounds.

Method

Where are your monuments, your battles, martyrs?
Where is your tribal memory? Sirs,
in that gray vault. The sea. The sea
has locked them up. The sea is History.

~Derek Walcott

In 2004 I began interviewing a Black, male dramatist as part of a project that would continue over seven years. The other three male artists were interviewed in 2005, 2006, 2007, and 2010. Each of the artists was chosen because of his extensive experience as a professional in his chosen field in the arts and his long involvement with training young artists at institutions of higher education. My intention was to meet each scholar once a year for three years and find out what they had been doing as teachers in their field. I managed to keep to that schedule of meeting three times over three years for three of the artists. The final participant was out of touch for three years while he built his consulting business away from higher education. When I finally connected with him in 2010, he was again employed in higher education and was building a lighting design program for a university in the Caribbean.

The Setting

These male artists principally operate in two countries and four states in the USA. The dancer/choreographer is a faculty member at a college for the arts in southern USA. The lighting designer was employed at a university in Midwest USA when I did two of his three interviews between 2005 and 2007. He then left the USA and began working as a consultant in the Caribbean and several states in the USA. He also did work in Brazil and a few European countries by the time I completed his final interview in 2010. The musician/composer is still employed as full-time faculty in a state on the eastern coast of the USA. Finally, the dramatist is now retired from his position at a leading arts institution in Canada. He has published a book on the folk traditions of his native island.

The Participants

Four Black, male artists teaching in higher education were the participants in this study. Two of the men were full-time, tenured faculty, one was full-time non-tenured faculty, and one was retired and held emeritus status at the time of my interviewing for the project. One of the scholars was married to a White American, and two had children. All four traveled and studied outside of their native country and the USA; two listed their master's degree as the final formal education certification; one completed his undergraduate degree and was involved in more academic training; one completed professional development courses while he was pursuing his professional career. All four of the scholars included outreach in the community as part of their ongoing commitments. None of these artists worked with each other before migrating from their original homes in the Caribbean to the USA. They knew of each other and recalled instances when their names were mentioned as part of professional productions at different points over the years. Participants were given pseudonyms and were invited to write the biographies that described them as presented below.

Leo, the dancer/choreographer, was founder, president, and artistic director of his dance theater company. He began his dance training before he turned 12 under the guidance of the elders of the Yorubas. He was trained as artistic director, teacher, mentor, and choreographer in the Folk Dance Group, for which he won awards and prizes for best dancer and choreographer in the national arts competition. Leo went on to win the first Prize for Outstanding Leadership and Achievement in Dance at his alma mater in New York and danced with four leading companies in that city. For the past 13 years he has served as mentor, choreographer, and coach for many winners of the National Foundations for the Arts Competition, at the dance school where he teaches. Hugo is a globally recognized master teacher and choreographer in modern dance and the African dance retentions of his native country.

Hugo was active in theatre as actor, dancer, director, choreographer, teacher, and producer. He was also a full professor of theatre arts at a university from which he retired as Professor Emeritus. He has written extensively and given lecture demonstrations on the history, dance, movement, chants, and theatrical forms of the traditional masquerade characters in Carnival.

Richard, the musician/composer, is a bassist, steel drummer, and an Associate Professor. He began his professional career in 1978 as a bassist for a calypsonian in his native island and has since recorded and performed with some of that island's leading artists, singers, and composers. The musician has conducted a youth steelband orchestra at an International Youth Music Festival and has been a member of a national theatre workshop, as well as a national television workshop. His compositions include theme music for six television productions, one of which was an award-winning program. He was musical director for a Nobel Prize winner's month long run of a production in the USA; recorded with state-based groups, and performed with nationally recognized jazz artists. He continues to freelance as a bassist apart from playing with his own band and sharing his talents with two other performing groups. He has recorded two CDs to date.

Gerard, the lighting designer, is an Associate Professor and began his career as a stagehand for a leading dance company in Trinidad. His journey in the performing arts has taken him into stage management, properties management, theatre management, costume design, set design, lighting design, and directing and producing for the theatre. As an educator he has taught at universities in the Caribbean, northeastern USA, and southeastern USA. He has 25 years of experience in higher education teaching at graduate and undergraduate levels, and administration. His research interests include emerging lighting technology, new plays, women designers in the mas [masquerade of the Caribbean], and puppet design and fabrication.

Data Collection

Case study research is an investigation of a bounded system (Merriam, 1988). It is a description and analysis of a single unit. Stake (2000) would describe the stories of these artists in the project as a collective case study representing multiple cases of a phenomenon, which makes "a more compelling argument" for the importance of the situation being investigated (Barone, 2004, p. 9). I have followed Patton's (1990) advice and sought "information rich" (p. 169) participants to help me understand the experiences of successful Black, male scholars in academia.

The study developed inductively with categories and questions emerging from the data provided by four male artists in their three interviews. After every interview, each participant was given a copy of an audio cassette with the interview and a transcript. Videotapes of two interviews were kept by the researcher and copied for the artists so that they could hold on to their own records. Two scholars were not video taped on the third interview because they were out of the country. The professors were asked to review the audiotapes and written documents to ensure that no words were left out and that the spelling of specialized vocabulary was included on the transcript. They could remove any information they did not want to have reported. They could also add in bold typeface any information that they thought was important to clarify a point that they had made during one of the three interviews. The professors could also highlight any quotes that they did not want to be used in the final report. Participants only corrected titles, technical terms, and then returned transcripts to me.

The Interview Protocol

When I began the interviews with the four artists in the study, I had three broad questions in mind (Seidman, 1991). During the first interview with Richard, Leo, Gerard, and Hugo the questions included the following. How did you come to be a professor at your institution? I followed up with a prompt like the one that I asked the lighting designer: "Tell me in as much detail as you can muster how you came to be a lighting designer to get to this point in your journey, stopping at any point and going through any series of events in detail." I wanted to find out as much as possible about his life leading up to his present position, to his status as a Black man with a career in the performing arts, and his history of teaching. Next, I asked about the details of a day in his life as an artist and teacher in his position? I added prompts such as: "If you had to train an actor to portray you, what would be the menu that they would have to become familiar with?" I wanted to find out about the kinds of activities that would fill his daily round. Finally, I asked about his experience as a Black man with a career in the arts and education and what it meant to him. Prompts included, for example, "When you look back on your book of life, this journey called professor of music is a chapter, tell me what it means to you in the context of all the other chapters?"

The second year when I met with Richard and Leo, and spoke with Hugo on the phone because he was in another country, I wanted to find out what had been going on during the year that we had not talked. For Hugo, there was one question: "Okay, could you cover the information that you thought was missing from the first interview?" His answer filled the entire hour that we continued on the phone. For the dancer/ choreographer, Leo, the initial question was: "And now I am going to ask you to tell me the highlights of the last year as a teacher and artist." I referenced the first interview from the previous year to frame this question: "Now, last year you told me that your work with the students based on interest and knowing their background, how did each solo connect to the student who did the solo?" This helped Leo to make clear to me his history as a teacher and the details of how his career connected with the events that were taking place in the present interview.

The final year that I did interviews with the professors, I wanted to catch up with events that had taken place over that year in three cases, and with Gerard I had to find out what had gone on during the previous three years that he had not been in touch with me. Questions to all the artists included: (a) "what have been the highlights this year . . . from June last year to June this year?" (b) "Talk about your highlights as a teacher," and (c) "tell me about . . . any students or any performance, any star moments where you as a teacher felt . . . it's coming together."

Interviews With the Colleagues and Friends

Each of the artists in the project gave me a list of two to three colleagues, or friends, whom they considered "the closest people on the journey as artist and teacher" who they were describing to me. The dancer/choreographer included two teachers from his dance training experience and a schoolmate who went on to become a company member in one of the dance organizations where they were both employed. Richard, the musician/composer included two people. One was a band member who spent many years as a performer with the musician. He also asked me to speak with a colleague who performed on his first CD and was a long-time associate from his days as a college student. Gerard, the lighting designer chose three female colleagues from different times in his career. The first was trained by the designer when he was a manager of a theater on his home island. The other two women were professors at one of the colleges where the lighting artist taught and did designs for shows on the campus. Finally, Hugo, the dramatist asked me to speak with his student, wife, and two colleagues. One had managed, the other performed in his acting company at different points in his career as a director.

The protocol for each of the interviews with the friends and colleagues who agreed to speak with me about the artists in the project included questions like: (a) Could you begin by telling me a little bit about yourself so I know who I'm talking with at this point in time? (b) Could you give me your perspective on his journey as an artist and teacher? (c) Are there highlights that stick out to you along this journey that you have observed? (d) Do you know what his life is like now that he is a . . . professor at [a university]? (e) You've been around his students and company members who have worked with him; what's the reputation; what's the word on [him]? (f) You've seen him perform for many years. Can you talk about that experience? (g) If you had to prepare a student or company member to work with him, what would be on the bullet list that you made sure that you passed on to him? (h) When you look back on your life, this chapter called "[your colleague] as an artist and a teacher" fits in and could you talk about where it fits and why? (i) Any last thoughts or feelings about this journey called, "[my colleague] as the Artist and Teacher" that you want to share with me?

Integrity Measures

I followed Lincoln and Guba's (1985) recommendations for data analysis: triangulation, prolonged engagement, peer debriefing, member checks, and thick description. Triangulation was achieved by the collection of the interviews with the male artists, the review of publications, applications for grants, interviews with various journals and newspapers, and service reports that they shared in emails, and the cross-referencing of information provided in the separate accounts of the career in the arts by each professor. Prolonged engagement was conducted through the constant communication with the men beginning in February 2004 through 2011, after several versions of the final report on the findings had been written, and edited videos representing the patterns across the artists' interviews were shared with the professionals. The participants also reviewed drafts of the chapters on each case study for this book. Changes were made where clarity was improved by the artists' input.

Peer debriefing began with members checking transcripts of the interviews for errors and places where more information would help to improve their answers to prompts. The names of people and places were changed so that they could not be easily identified if the transcripts got into the wrong hands by accident or misadventure. This process continued when participants saw the edited video productions that were created to represent the patterns that evolved in the cross-case analysis as they discussed their experiences in performance and teaching. Member checks were done as the video tapes of the interviews with each artist were reviewed by the participants and comments were shared with the researcher concerning anything that was to be removed from the tapes.

Finally, thick description was completed in the writing that was done to present the backgrounds, formative experiences, and journeys through the performing and professional careers in each artist's field to the present position as teacher that each scholar now occupies in their career. These stories represent the collective picture that has been drawn to describe "a converging line of inquiry" (Yin, 1994, p. 92).

Videotaping allowed the artists to see the body language that accompanied their comments so that they recalled the attitude in which they shared their experiences. This was an important form of documentation to refer to when (a) the transcripts of the interviews; and (b) the final written reports on the study were presented for the artists' review. When an artist did not recall saying something in a specific context, they were asked to refer to the transcript, the audio recording, and the video recording of the particular interview in order to reconstruct the register of their comment and the way that it was expressed to the interviewer. Trust in the researcher's perceptions of unstated insights or residual emotions about an episode that was recounted by the artist was easy to establish once this protocol of referencing all the forms of documentation was used to establish the integrity of the story in each case study.

Data Analysis

After reading the transcripts of the audiotaped interviews, a preliminary coding based on emerging themes was completed. Next, a process of constant comparison (Strauss & Corbin, 1990) was used to compile the findings and coordinate initial codes for each of the interviews. Then the interview transcripts for each participant and their network were reanalyzed to confirm categories, make final changes, and cull the titles that would be used to represent the data themes. Each case was presented under four general themes, that is, background of the participant, the character traits that are represented in the comments by the artist and their network, the philosophy that they espouse about creating products in their particular field, and finally, the teaching experiences that they and their network participants describe. During the second review of the transcripts for each of the artists, close attention was paid to the descriptions of the five areas of the core of imagination-intellectual development (Weems, 2003), that is, aesthetic appreciation, oral expression, written expression, performance, and social consciousness. These components form the rubric that organizes the daily work lives of the scholars, and the creative projects in the classrooms and community that each participant and their network members described in the interviews.

In Their Own Words

"Once you've mastered that vocabulary, there are no rules, you know?
You can just tell your story. And you can help other people tell their stories.
And you can tell your stories together and start communicating on a unified level."
~Esperanza Spalding (as cited by Soeder, 2011)

Conversations with these artists, fellow islanders, have opened my eyes to new ways of looking at them. In three of the cases, I have known the men at least 30 years. In one case, I have been in communication with the artist for barely 7 years. I would not otherwise have been privy to the artists' intimate ideas about creativity and the role that teachers must play in the lives of young people who want to become members of the "theater club" to which the practitioners belong.

There are phrases and paragraphs from the interviews carried out since 2004 that stay in my mind. Long after I have finished the interview, read the transcript, and reviewed the video recording that we made, I have a lingering feeling about the artists' insights on the way that they make art and communicate with the rest of the world. I feel that each of the artists reveals himself in a particular way that must be understood in the context of the many years that it has taken for the individual to find the symbols to articulate his vision of an ideal art. Throughout the interviews the men made me feel that they were laying themselves bare as they talked about their early beginnings as artists, the creative processes that they have evolved through trial and error, and their profound connection with their students.

I offer some excerpts from our conversations here in order to reveal the nature of the insights that I gleaned and to introduce the artists who I describe in subsequent chapters.

Leo the Dancer/Choreographer.
I'll always be trying to work on my creative process as a choreographer and just making my own spiritual connection in terms of how I express myself,

spiritually, through the art of dancing and choreographing . . . and use myself as a conduit to have the dancers' voices be heard, because usually that's not the case. It's the choreographer's sole purpose . . . getting his or her thing out, but always . . . I've always tried to have the dancers have a voice.

Gerard, the Lighting Designer/Manager.
[Designing] still comes down to you, a paper, and a pencil, and some angel telling you this is cool, this is okay, what you've planned. Because you get to that moment and I guess, just like a painter, the empty canvas, something has to happen there. . . . That's where you hope that everything that you've lived for, that you've done before, [leads to] equally good choices. I think any artist about to do a new work goes through that same fear because you know it's a blank piece of paper, and where do you start, what goes on that piece of paper first? That's the strange part because you just hope for inspiration, sometimes it certainly may not be you, it is some sort of . . . if you want to call it chan-neling, if you want to call it divine inspiration, something else is coming into play at that point.

Richard, the Musician/Composer.
It's hard for [some people] to get you out of, you know, out of "this is the box," this singular tradition [of playing an instrument] that you're supposed to be proficient in and what people do. . . . I hope [my career is] not [about] being just jack of all trades and, and master of none. It's really about not limiting yourself to any one thing and I think the more you stretch yourself, you see where things connect. You see other relationships and you hold on to those relationships and explore what are the similarities in these different things that you do.

Hugo, the Dancer/Dramatist.
We have to write our plays, brother, because we are human beings like any-body else and some of the things that are happening in [our country] are hap-pening in other countries of the world and even our writers, I know our poets, write about those in human terms . . . we are writing for everybody. One of the problems I had when I was doing my theatres . . . and I was selecting plays from [our island was that] they were so culturally specific that it meant nothing to the people, to the Black [North Americans] sitting in the audience . . . and I didn't want to speak to such [a limited group].

                    Hugo

Huge
                Energy personified
                            Eyes alert
To everything   Inside and outside
The Universe   No lines
            No end to
                    Horizon
                                Only space
Time   Movement
Endless   River coursing
To other
                Time
                        Places
                            People

Hugo   Human
Intense   Alive
Quivering   With electricity
And
Being
                Soul.

Chapter Two

Hugo's Horizons

Hugo remembers being recruited to do a play in his elementary school when he was seven years old. His teacher, the aunt of a man who later became a famous politician, invited "this child to take part in a play" that she was writing. Not only was Hugo the youngest person in the play, but he recalled that "anything they asked me to do, I jumped up and did it." "They continued re-writing and re-writing my part until I had just a big enough part, I was singing in it, I was dancing in it," and most importantly to the performer, he remembered having "no fear." Of all the performances that he has completed over a lifetime in the theater, he explained that "I have played and stood in front of audiences and got ovations in many parts of the world and I don't think any of that has struck me to the extent as . . . that first experience."

Growing up in a household with nine siblings, two by his father before he was married and the rest by both his parents, Hugo learned from the experience of watching plays being written and produced by a club that his brothers and sisters created. As Hugo reflected on his early home life, he said that his siblings "were all brothers and sisters to me. And it was a very close relationship from all; in fact I think my sisters were my second mother." The professor emeritus recollected that there was "always singing and dancing in my home, always celebrations, for Carnival particularly, Christmas, and the New Year." As a young boy, he was accustomed, he elaborated, to seeing his father and mother doing many dances and learned about the rehearsal process from watching the organization of productions unfold in his living room. He smiled when he reminisced about the fact that his "father let me stay up to take a look" at the rehearsals, but it was his mother who was the leader of the home. As he chuckled, he said that his father "was the voice and [his mother] was the force behind the voice" in the home.

Hugo performed in one play that was produced by his brother's club. It was an original play about a young boy who was "saved" by members of the Salvation Army. He remembered being given a monologue about "the value of Christianity and goodness." After that show, Hugo and his own friends decided that they would produce their plays apart from his older siblings. He described the excitement of going downtown to a popular store near his home and buying two one-act plays for the newly formed club.

The young director was responsible for the mounting of the productions "Philosophy and Petticoats" and "The Professor." Hugo played the professor in the latter and a philosopher in the former. What was most memorable about the second play, he related, was the fact that his friends played a trick on him during the production. Hugo explained that his fellow actor in a major scene

> . . . got all tangled in this chicken coop [that his other friends had placed in his way backstage] and here I am adlibbing and doing all kinds of things on stage and it's time for him to make his entrance and he's no where to be seen and I did all kinds of stage business. . . . I knew that he was going to come in some time and my friend came in all bedraggled, some feathers on him, and torn and a little bleeding, but he was gung-ho enough to still come in and do his part and I didn't bat an eye.

The reviewer of the show, according to Hugo, did not know that anything had gone awry with the production. In fact, his report in the newspapers later on talked about the production without any mention of the 'bedraggled" actor who came onstage.

This need to go on with the show, regardless of obstacles backstage, was a lesson that Hugo took into his professional life. He has had to explain to his theater students today and professionals in the productions that he has mounted that the show goes on no matter what happens on or off stage. What's more, Hugo insisted, it is even better if the audience is none the wiser if any miscalculation takes place in spite of the best intentions of the plans laid down during rehearsals.

Hugo described himself in the teen years as an "athlete" who "did track and field . . . played table tennis . . . played basketball, soccer, and cricket." He had tremendous energy and was popular among many social clubs and dance groups across the city where he lived. His talent for organizing was already apparent when he went to a Catholic priest to ask permission to use the church premises for his football team to meet on a regular basis. This club was organized with young men who were mostly described as immigrants from Grenada and he was actually referred to as a Grenadian himself at one point in his youth. His outgoing nature and his ability to cross easily from one social strata to another became the foundation for his success in the area of the performing arts that was part of the social scene at other venues on the island.

His wife, Felicia, described Hugo as someone who "barely graduated from high school" and one with "training in theatre and dance" based on his experience of performing with amateur groups around the city. Hugo's long list of credentials as a dancer, Felicia suggested, could be ascribed to the fact that "he does things without any formal training. He just does them because he gets interested and he moves with it." Hugo's wife, along with a mentee who has known Hugo for some twenty years, said that the dramatist and director was "basically a self-taught person." In fact, Bernard, the mentee who met Hugo in Canada, described his mentor as a "professional artist without the traditional academic qualifications." This experience was gained through Hugo's long years of commitment with the Root Theater and his performance education under the leader, Miss Mack, who was later known as the mother of Caribbean dance.

Hugo's name is now mentioned along with Caribbean men of achievement in the ranks of Derek Walcott, "Geoffrey Holder . . . and the late Dr. Errol Hill," according to his longtime associate and mentee, and is appreciated for what he "did for drama" and Black professional theater in Canada. Hugo's mentee, Bernard, remembered attending a lecture by the dance leader of the Root Theater, Miss Mack, who "used storytelling to support her integrated and geometric folk movement demonstrations" and "Hugo's name was mentioned so often during that day, it stuck in my mind. I then always wanted to know "who was [th]is Hugo boy?" that was highly regarded by the mother of Caribbean dance.

In an environment in which all theatre was done at an "amateur" level, Hugo was not paid but established himself as a celebrated dancer, even as "he was struggling working as a daily paid worker clerk of some sort on the docks on his native island," according to his wife, Felicia. However, when they decided to get together, their plan was to go to London and establish their relationship as Hugo continued in theater and Felicia followed her academic career at a university. Hugo had high hopes of continuing his performing career in London at that time.

Hugo and Felicia lived in London for nearly two years and were married there. He found himself in school doing dance and drama classes while his wife attempted to find work in academia.

He took "whatever jobs came his way" in the performing area, reported Felicia. A decision to apply for and eventually accept, a "Canada fellowship that was available at the time," led the couple to a new adventure where work in "various places in Canada in theater" was the beginning of the move away from performing for Hugo. They also spent some time in New York City where their son was born but the couple knew that they didn't want their son to grow up and "fight in anyone's army" as an American citizen, even though they were deeply involved in the Civil Rights Movement and understood the need to be a part of the changing social scene in the USA.

They decided to remain in Canada and Felicia recalled that Hugo "worked . . . at the Classical Theater festival . . . and then he got hired at the Montréal Theater to teach at the New School." After many successful years in Montreal, Hugo's final move in Canada was to the School of Theater Arts in Toronto. Felicia intimated that she believed Hugo "is good at what he does," which is why he was hired as an associate professor in Toronto, and that his career was devoted to creating "different strategies to teach physical movement to actors—which sort of combines his two interests in dance and drama."

Hugo pointed out that he was always aware that he "was working in Canada at a time when . . . it was difficult for anybody of color, blacks, Chinese, Indians . . . to enter the country. And there were only specific conditions [for any exception]." His associates in Montréal "saw a loop hole in the law" that allowed him to be employed as someone with a "specialty" in theater that no one in Canada could provide. The reality of his situation as a Black immigrant did not discourage Hugo from establishing the first Black theater company in two cities. His wife pointed out that "for about ten years" Hugo "had a big struggle with the theaters, particularly in Toronto" and in spite of the challenges "that he achieved some gratification from that." In the midst of all of this production activity Hugo went on to become the head of the department at the School of Theater Arts. Bernard, Hugo's mentee from their native island, was also quick to point out that Hugo was quickly promoted to full professor in "one of the most innovative universities in the country and by extension in the world."

Hugo's Moments in the Light

The years that Hugo spent building up his career as a dancer and leader in his native island are still remembered by those who knew the founders of dance as a discipline among the folk arts practitioners. Hugo recalled one choreographer with whom he performed early on in his dance career as one who "wanted people of experience, people with stage presence, people of maturity, and that's the reason why I think she sent for me and talked to me and I came in to participate in the show." Bernard, Hugo's mentee, was trained by a fellow from Hugo's Root Theater days, so he was always reminded by this teacher that Hugo was a trailblazer on the local dance scene on the island. In his dancing days Hugo was reputed to be "somebody that was very physical" and a good actor. As Bernard recalled the importance of his association with the legacy of the pioneers of folk performers, "the Root Theatre is where the seeds of concert Dance Theatre in [our island] were sown," and Hugo's name is synonymous with that movement and its continued importance among the dancers on the island and abroad.

Tours to other Caribbean islands and North America, particularly Canada, with the Root Theater members were a major part of the experience that Hugo accumulated as a performer. In Jamaica, he worked closely with dancers who had far more training in ballet than he did, and he explained that "they were more dance oriented physically in terms of appearance and dress" but he was an advanced pupil in the folk arts forms of his native land. The seasoned dancer recalled introducing the "cake dance", a folk performance piece from his native island, to the audience as part of his island's presentation on a bill that featured works from all the Caribbean islands at a major festival. In another performance, where he was imitating a rooster who was interacting with a hen, he out danced his partner to the great amusement of his fellow cast members and the audience at the shows. Hugo reminisced about the way that he "owned this theater . . . [when he] brought my rooster into it." He smiled as he recollected that he and his partner "brought the house down" since the dance "was that good" as a result of the fact that both dancers "caught on fire" in front of the live audience.

In his early time in Canada he was asked to direct a section of a television special by a Canadian director. He recalled that the television producer showed "the script and he said, 'do you know a kid who dances to do this?'" to Hugo. It happened that Hugo was involved with some dancers from the local university who had asked him to mount a show for their "Carnival Week" festivities. As a result of the producer's request, Hugo organized a rehearsal with the university dancers so that the producer's crew could see what was being created for their show. The dancers were offered pay for their performances, but it was Hugo who chose the ones that he wanted to work with in the final production for the television company. He made sure that the less disciplined dancers were not chosen for the final presentation on television.

The veteran artist mentioned that he was "very offended" because he was not the leader making decisions on the way that the television show should be presented. However, he reminded himself that the production company was not "paying him" to produce, and that he would be better off if he paid attention to what the official producer was doing and find out "what he has to do." It brought back memories of the time when he and other dancers choreographed a piece and did not get any credit for their creative input. As the talented folk dancer recalled:

> We delivered the whole thing . . . he comes up like Lazarus and then he falls backward and instead of falling backward on the bed I come and I duck underneath him and he falls on my back and I carried him in a circle on my back and he is dancing backwards, it was theatrical as ever, and what really hurt us is that we never got credit for it.

The lesson of being overlooked when a performer has earned credit by hard work has ever remained in the forefront of Hugo's sense of justice and informed the way that performers should be honored for their creativity.

Staying Power

A vision of consistency remains in my mind after listening to Hugo and his four supporters talk about his path to the position of professor emeritus status. One of his mentees, Bernard, said that Hugo "would always advise me that when the down stroke comes, you never, ever look away from the target, even though you may feel like things are totally hopeless, you never look away from the target." It is a perspective that reverberates in the expression that Penny, another mentee from Hugo's theater production days, shared when she said that Hugo "stayed true to his feelings, never wavering. The Hugo that I met in the 1970s is the same Hugo today. . . . stronger in many areas as he grew and experienced but never, never wavered."

Another example of his consistency stemming from his early teen years in his native island came about through his association with social clubs and athletic teams across the city where he lived. He recalled holding meetings at his parish church when he was involved in a soccer club. While Hugo was not a staunch Catholic, like his mother and father, he did feel that he should be respectful to the priest because his family was so closely linked to the church and community. Hugo explained that his "mother and father were staunch believers, I respected them dearly, I disagreed [with the tenets of the church] . . . it was a gut feeling at the time, because I never explored why I was uncomfortable with Catholicism." The ability to maneuver in difficult situations, both with his growing discontent with his parents' church associations and the way in which social groups tried to tie him down to one strata of the society or the other, continued to serve him well as he traversed the cultural landscape on the island.

In another instance of his leadership skills, Hugo talked about his decision to go to the principal of his primary school, Mr. Jules, and ask for permission to stage a play with his drama group. Because of Hugo's solid reputation as a student and athlete, he was told "by all means, you're Hillary's son" and that was the way in which he got to stage his first dramatic productions in a public venue. This was further proof to the young man that his father was in good standing in the church and community in spite of the fact that Hugo believed that his parents were "church people" and "zealots of the church."

By his own admission, Hugo admitted that he "had a very strong inner independence [and] that nobody owns this man." This was apparent as early as his first encounters with the politics that prevailed among dance groups in the city where he started his performing career. The appraisal of Hugo's character in the comment by Bernard, his mentee, included the fact that the dancer "has walked the [artist's] path and he is well aware of when, where and how the creative energy should be used." Through observing the results of Hugo's long experience in the performing arts and his strong sense of purpose in life, Bernard has also concluded that the professor emeritus is "quite sensitive about the way he uses his creative energies, and knows when to stop" working on a project.

In Hugo's estimation he is "a citizen of the world because . . . whatever I have to do must have universal appeal, for it to have real creative content, because it will resonate with anybody. Whether they speak the same language or not," and this makes it easy for him to make artistic decisions. He has gathered this perspective after visiting and working in many countries around the world, and is now content to say that "My [island] passport is for identification, I come in there I am one of you folks, I'm going, I need this to get out." This statement is made to emphasize the fact that geographical boundaries do not describe the person who is going between nations. Therefore, Hugo does not limit himself to territorial loyalties or cultural definitions of who he is. As far as Hugo is concerned, "invisible barriers . . . will block out very important things that one can experience," if you allow the national divisions to keep you out from experiencing people and life.

With this political perspective firmly in place, Hugo was able to reflect on his path to a full professorship at the university where he taught drama and movement to the end of his formal teaching career. The former professor elucidated on his understanding of the path he traveled to maturity as a creative being. Other professors and instructors in his department did not "have my strength, my vision . . . my philosophy, my sense of theater, my sense of the arts, my philosophy of life, my breath of living. . . . They went through the process as required while I was learning life," and that made the difference in the way that he worked with students, faculty, and professionals in the theater industry. Such an analysis by Hugo is reflected in Bernard's description of the retired professor when he first encountered him at the School of Theater Arts in Canada. Bernard enthused:

> I remember thinking that here was this tall Black alpha-male, a hunted lion on stilts, walking in rhythm like a moko-jumbie [stilt walker] unfettered amongst the Western hunters—be they students, the University Directorate or the cutthroat Arts Administrators with whom he had to interact in order to do his creative arts work in the city.

Hugo's strong identification with his native land and the cultural art forms that he learned while a young man performing at the Root Theater is shown in many of his comments. For one, it is manifested in his reaction to some of the attitudes that he had encountered among fellow artists in his home country. At one point he described his frustration with people who "are so silly" and cause "so much infighting and so much stupidity, and so much selfishness and so much insecurity" because they do not see the larger picture about the way their folk forms can enhance the world culture. Hugo ascribed his attitude to the negativity among his peers to the fact that he is "not insecure at all about who I am and what [my native country] is about." Because of his independent attitude and cosmopolitan experience beyond the island, the artist explained that it is "very difficult to live permanently [on the island] because . . . very quickly a lot of the poisons that I smell [in the way people treat each other] and all the attitudes I recognize, start to affect me in a negative way." He explained that "a lot of [negative] behavior I experienced began to surface and float." And therefore . . . "[I decided that] before it blows in my direction, [and I] have to ingest and inhale, I decide[d] . . . to leave" for his self-preservation.

Since Hugo "always wanted to give and to do things" and "wanted to come back and use that knowledge" for the good of his island's development, he took an opportunity to study "where some of [the countries beyond his island] have gone [with the mixing of various folk traditions]," so that he could "make connections for future references." This decision to improve his professional knowledge led him to embark on a journey that took him to several countries when he was quite young. A Rockefeller scholarship allowed him to study production so that he could better facilitate the tours that various local dance companies would be invited to participate in while he was a dancer on his native island. By looking at the ways in which different countries in the Caribbean and Latin America developed their folk forms and expressed their indigenous cultures on stage, he was able to better facilitate the process in which his native country developed their folk traditions for stage productions. He explained that what he " . . . wanted was to go through the Caribbean and South America and to study places . . . culture and the mixes, the Spaniards the Africans and the Indigenous people. And how those things are fused and how it's portrayed, and their art forms and the cultural blending and fusions."

Another scholarship led the young theater practitioner to a new country where he could answer the questions of "how do you run a big [dance] company like this? And what do you do [once you go on tour to another country]?" Hugo wanted to know the answers for the benefit of his country's arts community, and so he became "an artist in residence" at a television studio, a theater, and a school. He visited a television studio in one state where he "had the authority, [once he] met with the head producer . . . to go into anything that they were producing, but not just to see the shows as much as sitting in the production meeting and listen to the planning." This effort to learn theater and television production as an intern was based on Hugo's belief that his island home could develop an enriched cultural art form that, once presented, could "seduce the world" much like Jamaican reggae music has done.

He reflected on a government decision to create a "highly competitive 'first person across the post to win in orders like horse racing'" approach to the performing arts on his home island. In Hugo's estimation, the grassroots effort to develop the folk performing arts could have been organized in a more "creative" way. When he described his repulsion to the way that the folk arts were being used in the political arena, he expressed deep concern for the youth of the country in his comment that "Europe is the one who created all the mess [in our colonial society] . . . so if we don't investigate that part of us, the unanswered questions that some of our youth answered themselves" in their own cultural art forms, then the country has to take responsibility for the ways in which young people decide to deal with the results of the negligence of adults.

Hugo opined about "all the young people today that have lost their compass" and who "could have been in those [community arts programs] when they were doing all those outrageous things, outrageous acts because they don't know who they are, they have no identification, they have no sense of community." He emphasized the role of the arts in the preservation and development of a society and looked to the community leaders "who are in charge" to acknowledge "our very terrible history . . . coming out of slavery" and the need for us to direct our energies in positive cultural activities.

In another description of the way in which the colonial power had corrupted youth outside of his island home, and the proof of how this poison manifested itself, Hugo described some of the challenges that he encountered in teaching White students about movement that was inspired by African drum accompaniment. The artist described how students would do imitations of African movements in a mocking style even though "all the things I went through" in the class should have led them to be more respectful of his method and its African inspired rhythms. The movement teacher lamented that "it is in [their] head, it's in the head" and then reported that he "took that drum, put it in my office and I took a big plate from home and put a plant on it" so that no one could find it easily. When students and colleagues came by his office in the School of Theater Arts and asked, "when are you going to use that drum?" he would say to himself: "I will never use that drum again, I will never allow them to insult the drum with their stereotype of the Hollywood mythology after I spent a long time teaching them how to break [the dance movement] down." He believes that "they didn't do [the movement as he taught them to] because they were vicious and they were mean" spirited and he was clear about the fact that "that part of the exercise [for better coordination] I am not interested in changing."

Know Thyself

Very early on in Hugo's life he was aware that "if I tell you I am going to do something, I am going to do it," and that character trait has impressed others. Penny, who began her training as a volunteer in one of Hugo's theater groups, recalled the fact that "being the professional that I am today, it's [based on] looking at Hugo. Because I am so particular about the work that I do" as an event planner. She also emphasized the fact that when you work with Hugo "everything is all well organized and laid out properly and [there is] no confusion, everything is just running smooth," when a rehearsal starts. Penny was clear about the fact that "Not many people really understand Hugo [and his demand for attention to details]. Not many people could walk with Hugo because he's not going to let you get away with anything, and I mean the simplest thing he will jump all over you."

Based on his conviction that he would always "allow my ego to step aside when I see somebody has something that I've never thought about. That I could learn from," Hugo proceeded to develop his theater skills over many years in several countries. He recalled an incident from his early years as an amateur dancer in his home island where the director of the performance company mistreated the dancers and Hugo left the evening's presentation with the belief that there was "lack of respect for what I was doing. [I understood] very early that [we were thought to be] . . . dancing monkeys." It was that experience that led Hugo to vow to treat his art and performers with deep appreciation and respect. The concept that organizers of theater productions would have anything less than high regard for the dancers and actors in their charge was not understandable to Hugo.

Young Hugo's personality led to him being included in several dance groups across his home city. He remembered that "whenever little groups had some kind of celebration, they would ask me to participate and I participated" with anybody. The producers of these shows would say, "do this, do that, [and] I did it," without any reservation, so that there was never any disagreement or sense of him being subservient to anyone. This flexibility reflected the same attitude that guided him when he played with a soccer team from a neighborhood outside of the one where he grew up. Hugo explained his reason for joining the team, in spite of the fact that his own neighborhood crew thought that he was disloyal to them. He ruminated about the fact that the young players in the "guest" team "were fun to be with, it was a good team and whether or not they were in a higher [social] status than I [was], never crossed my mind."

Along the journey of his career, there were other judges of Hugo's character who played a significant role in his work as a professional artist. When it was time for Hugo to be promoted to professor at the School of Theater Arts, he reasoned that the decision was made by the Dean of the school. The committee initially voted to delay Hugo's promotion, but they were instructed by the dean to rethink their decision before sending their final letter with a vote to the head of the arts school. Hugo remembered the incident in detail and reflected on the fact that the Dean wrote a letter in which he talked about Hugo's "caliber" and the fact that he should be given the promotion because of his accomplishments. Hugo did not fully understand how the Dean could be so supportive of him when they had only dined together once, under very rushed circumstances. However, it was clear to the artist that the reputation of his work ethic was well established in the school and the professional community by the time that his promotion was under discussion.

By all reports from his former students, Penny and Bernard, Hugo was a stickler for discipline. He believed in teaching his students about "the philosophy of life and being gracious" and ensured that actors in his performing companies would conduct themselves in a professional manner. Hugo insisted that when actors came into "this space [to rehearse] that your garbage needs to be left outside" so that work is created in a reverential attitude. The director had always insisted that his students at the School of Theater Arts be aware that they could express their bad attitudes to "someone if you have issues with them," and this could only be possible if the students "know how to check themselves and how to play [in the theater space]." That was the only condition under which he would negotiate any negative feelings that seeped into work space in the theater.

Penny, the event planner, recalled a time when she was late getting to the theater to work with Hugo and his acting company. She remembered that the floor was not swept at the standard that the director expected from his stage crew. Even though Penny was then a volunteer, she was fearful that Hugo would shout at her and express his disappointment in her lack of understanding of the need for the space to be ready for the actors. Hugo told Penny in no uncertain terms that "you can't have . . . performers coming here and this floor isn't perfect," because it is a sign of disrespect for the work that would be created in that space. To this day she finds herself holding others to the same standard that she learned from Hugo when she was with his company of performers. Penny believes that this work ethic has ensured her good reputation across the city when she is in charge of a production as an event specialist.

Hugo upheld the same high standard for himself when he was being interviewed for a promotion at the School of Theater Arts after 10 months at the organization. He explained to the dean "what I intend to do and how I was taught things should be done." Penny, Hugo's theater associate, witnessed the fact that Hugo's lifetime commitment was not only about the practical application of high standards in theater arts, but about "trying his best" to "bring [his island's cultural traditions] back" and that his work has always followed the line of belief that "if he shared what he's doing on a regular basis, eventually it might seep into a number of people who had tried their best to keep this [folk form] alive because of it's importance to our own country."

Teaching for Posterity

When Hugo began his teaching journey, he was certain that he "could be a change agent" when he returned to his native country. He knew that he "was going to be an educator" and he "didn't have to go to be a doctor, a lawyer or anything like this." He admitted that when he was initially offered the position of associate professor at a university, he didn't know what that meant in practical terms. However, it is still a surprise to him that he turned out to be a "university professor." The professor emeritus also knew that he would work "through the art of the culture because I think that's where the markers should be laid and put down" so that his native country's history could be documented and disseminated.

The work that Hugo did with the Root Theater on his home island was principally guided by his mentor Miss Mack. One of the main discussions that informed Hugo's approach to teaching the folk forms of dance that he learned when studying and performing with Miss Mack was the impact that ballet training had on the local dancers. Concerned about the "mind-set" that altered when the women, in particular, took ballet classes, Hugo explained that it seemed that "they did 2 classes and they felt . . . like Charlie Chaplin . . . 'cause in ballet . . . the balance [of the body] is done differently." This was of particular concern to the theater pioneer, Miss Mack, because she explained that she could not "understand why a young woman or a young man who is born and grow up [on the island] cannot undulate" after taking a few ballet classes. In Hugo's analysis of the situation he could say that the dancers " . . . don't see that the things that they do naturally, that they can do creatively, that come from out of their own sense of who they are and what they experience in their lives, that they can transfer that to stage."

By the time that Hugo arrived at the School of Theater Arts, where he was to be tenured and promoted to the position of full professor, he "was pulling things from modern dance . . . pulling things from jazz, . . .

pulling things from all aspects of art. But the foundation, the concept, the philosophy came out of my own background from [my dance experience on the island]." Hugo believed that "he made those connections as a child" that ensured that he did not end up with a "divided" mind that would "inhibit the juices from flowing" when he went on stage. He still gives his thanks to Miss Mack for taking the cultural forms "from the canals as people treated [it] and put [the folk dance] on the sidewalk, at least, and gave it some respect." This "unconsciously searching for that respect" for his island's culture was one of the reasons that Hugo chose to follow the path that his mentor, Miss Mack, articulated for him.

The impact of Miss Mack's influence on Hugo's relationship with his own students is reflected in the way that he built rapport with them over his teaching career. In one reflection on his teaching journey, Hugo explained that "I used to tell them . . . don't respect me because I am the professor and I am the teacher . . . we are here for one reason and when you enter that door it is a common love and respect and that is sacred for me." The high level of expectation for his students' development that Hugo expressed in this mantra is also echoed in Bernard's review of the impression that his mentor made on others who worked on productions or studied with the movement coach. Bernard, the young dance student who sought out Hugo at the School of Theater Arts, said:

> I would contend that only those who are able to deal with Hugo's multilayered complexity can relate to him comfortably. Others will eventually shy away because they are not able to really sustain the energy, much less the momentum that he requires for engagement. And this is not just because Hugo wants it, but because nature demands it.

When Hugo related a story about one of his students who was mounting a production of *For Colored Girls Only* by Ntozake Shange, he was clear about the fact that the student had to be reminded that she was principally a director and that she would be graded on her directing ability. He recounted that he advised the young, Black woman to " . . . . find a common ground [with the White, female actors]. They're all women. Abused women [in the society] is not a Black phenomenon, you know, they must have aunts and mothers and sisters who have had bad relationships, or they themselves with their boyfriends."

He further encouraged the female students to "sit together in a circle of women and plug into that part of it [about the abuse by men] and you're home free. All the other things of the blackness. . . . Let them apply that to their experiences." The student took Hugo's advice and completed the exercise successfully. This was yet another example of Hugo's lived experience at work. To quote him, he had the advantage of doing "all these [theater] experimentations without a book, without looking at anybody's stuff. I drew these things out of my own [native country's] background, tying it all from my knowledge of the world and things that I see. Pulling from other areas" to make a distinctive theater style.

One of Hugo's memories about explaining his teaching stance to students is documented in his recollection of a speech that he often made to his charges at some point in the program with him. Based on his experience at the Theater School where he began teaching "the stage movements, physical presence" and other theater skills, Hugo had evolved a perspective on his role in a theater student's life. The artist would explain to the young stewards: "I don't care how you feel towards me but I assure you when I come to this space I am prepared for anything. I . . . believe I know my stuff, what I don't know I am not teaching . . . and so what I am teaching you I know very well . . . it is something about life."

Bernard, the young dancer who sought out Hugo's counsel while he was in school, echoed this perspective from Hugo in his comment about the conversations that he held with the professor over an extended period of time. Now a movement specialist, Bernard reflected on:

> the wide-ranging research Hugo was involved in re: the Carnival, and . . . the experiences of other artistes he admired, including the late [a famous folk dancer], [one of Jamaica's leading dancers and choreographers] and the [nationally acclaimed sisters from his island] just to mention a few . . . or the extensive international research project Hugo completed with the support of his wife Felicia while fulfilling a prestigious Rockefeller scholarship.

Felicia, Hugo's wife of more than four decades, mentioned the fact that there are many actors in Canada who were former students of her husband's while he was teaching and directing in Canada. Hugo, who admitted that he "really love[d] young people," talked about the fact that he was always welcomed to one theater school where he interacted with actors as "an idea person, because I brought my island stuff, my English stuff" and all the other training, including what he learned from his first foreign teacher who "used to use her body . . . [so that] . . . everything was dramatic, it wasn't just straight dance" informed by ballet values.

It is a fact, Felicia commented, that "so many students that are still around [Canada] . . . have been influenced by [Hugo] and taught by him," at the university or at the theater school that hired Hugo before he joined academia. Bernard, the movement specialist, believes that Hugo's influence is partially due to the master teacher's "intuition and self-confidence, the power of his words, his sense of perfect self-expression—to get what he wanted" in his teaching career and his work as a director. It is also true, Bernard emphasized, that it was due to the support of Hugo's wife and family. Hugo's "vision of theater, of the carnival integrated into the folk form," is one of the principal reasons that he has had such an important role in the training of theater students.

Hugo's reference to a lecture demonstration where he "put on the [carnival] music and everybody danced . . . jumped up and down," and the fact that "nobody ever did that" at a formal lecture/demonstration, was all innovative in the 1960s when he was just breaking into the Canadian theater scene. Further, the fact that his movement classes at a particular national institute included classes for the actors "with a drum [as accompaniment]," grounded in the African aesthetic that he had studied and performed under the direction of Miss Mack, "was touching [the actors'] internal, primal . . . nerve endings" and pushing them to new levels of artistic expression at the national program.

After many years of teaching, directing, and presenting lectures on the folk forms from his native country to international audiences, Hugo was invited to present on the home island along with other luminaries who had spent a lifetime studying and documenting the folk forms of their island. Bernard, a prime mover in the organization of the memorable event, reminisced about Hugo's role in the "presentations . . . on Carnival in collaboration with cultural luminaries such as [Professor Pat], [a nationally celebrated poet] and [the founder of the arts center at a university campus on the island]." This is yet another instance of the standard of excellence with which Hugo was identified. This fact was reflected in the comment by Gerard, Hugo's theater colleague, that "Hugo was a trail blazer in Canada" when no Black theater institutions were in existence and has remained the standard to which others work to attain.

The esteem in which Hugo was held in Canada and his homeland was further reflected in Penny's comment about her gratitude for the times that she has spent with Hugo over their many years of association. The event planner described her feeling that "Anytime you sit with Hugo you learn something. It could be something really tiny but you always come home with, 'Ah! I didn't know that.' . . . I love the teacher part of him." In further support of her analysis of life with her mentor, Penny described the relationship that Hugo has developed with her daughter who is now performing with an international company.

Penny didn't realize that her daughter and Hugo "were that close" until Hugo explained at one point in time that the young woman was "in New York," and that "she did the Lion King in Toronto and then she got a short Broadway [part] but she's in New York." Penny understood that the foundation of the relationship between Hugo and her daughter was based on the fact that "she's a singer, dancer, actor," and this was why Hugo and her daughter "connected." The proud mother also recalled that her mentor had given "some of his history books" to the young performer. Penny is happy that the two artists have a growing relationship and that her daughter "has a bond with [Hugo] now" since she knows "where his head is at."

There are criticisms, or cautions, that his longtime associates share when they talk about working with Hugo. The insights about the master teacher were mentioned by all four of the participants who agreed to be interviewed for this project. Bernard, the movement specialist, talked about Hugo's "no-nonsense approach" to life and his work in the theater. He iterated that "While there are those who will relate to Hugo fairly easily (I do, since I too am a no-nonsense person) there are obviously those who will be intimidated by his way of doing things. So they will see him as a threat, because he just doesn't tolerate crap."

Penny, the event specialist, pointed out that "to be the best I can at what I am doing to meet up with Hugo [and his expectations], I had to be extremely good at delivering. That was the challenge for me [as a member of his theater group.] It is that [discipline under Hugo that has] help[ed] me be the person I am today in terms of anything that I touch." Penny admitted that she was "afraid" of Hugo in their earliest days in the acting company that Hugo directed.

While Hugo intimated that he was "only sensitive to students who are there and make themselves available" to learning, it is obvious that he has a very high standard that must be met if a person is going to be counted among the deserving in his classroom. Bernard revealed that Hugo and the other teachers who came out of the experience of Miss Mack's grounding in theater on the island are "the personifications of true professionalism and the highest of standards." Bernard further explained that to work successfully with the seasoned artist "you must be honest with yourself. Prof. Hugo (excuse my French) is not a 'bullshitter'."

The movement specialist also explained how he matured his perspective on his role as a theater artist under the guidance of Hugo. He pointed out that "prior to [following the Professor's directions], I tended at times to be the typical soft-hearted [island] artiste 'cleaning ground for monkey to run on' for the symbolic two hops-bread and cheese with a sweet drink as reward." The result of his transformation at the Hands of Hugo, and life experience, is that Bernard can keep his "eye on the target, both financially and spiritually" and provide for his family.

Another of Hugo's longtime associates, Gerard, intimated that when he was a student at the School of Theater Arts, it was Hugo who "was able to guide me through some of my rough political waters because, as you may know, even in academic institutions, there is a great deal of politics." This former student, and acting company member, recalled the fact that Hugo " . . . was always available for consultation even though he was not directly one of my prof[essor]s. But it was good to know that there was someone there, someone to whom I could speak in confidence knowing that the person would be more interested in seeing you do well than having my trust betrayed to other professors and students."

This peer of some thirty-two years also attested to the fact that Hugo is "able to set a goal, focus on it, and . . . complete a task" once he's started a journey. Although Gerard believes that Hugo "is a very private man" and that he worked under a lot of stress during two of the dramatic productions that he mounted in Toronto, he never let on to company members that his life was under considerable pressure. This is testimony to the fact, in Gerard's eyes, that Hugo is "very loyal and . . . able to function under stress in a very effective way." Finally, Gerard had to mention the fact that he felt privileged to have won Hugo's friendship after a long probation period. He stated: "I think that it's safe to say there's a friendship there" after all these years of interaction as artists and the trials that both men have survived in a predominantly White society far from their island home.

Leo

A lion
Sitting on   His throne
Sending out
Rays
Of light
To all
who
People his

                              Domain
Power
Beauty
Love   Intense devotion
Pushing
Probing
Healing
Demanding

Leo   Lion
Lord   Of all
He surveys

Chapter Three

Leo's Journey

Leo's story begins in a small island in the English speaking Caribbean. As he described his initiation into the dance world, he started out in a "converted pig pen" which had "no covering [except] a plum tree" and this same tree provided him with plums "in between [rehearsing the] sequence of the movements" for the dances. When the rain stopped, and the drummers came out from sheltering under the plum tree, everyone had to wait for the sun "to dry the dug up concrete rivers" that criss-crossed the small plot where the rehearsals were conducted. It was at this site where Leo fed bananas to the pigs that he broke his ankle "in those holes" at a young age. He explained his evolution in to the dance arena in this way:

> I wanted to . . . play piano and I wanted to be the one guy who brings the music out. But my parents didn't have the twenty-five cents to pay for the weekly fees for my piano lessons and so I had to abandon that and ended up in the [prayer palaces] because I heard music [coming from there]. So I went, I followed wherever the music went, I followed. And I think that's the same thing for my dancing. I am only inhibited by the requirements of the technique, the particular style of movement that I have to produce and the way I [have to produce] the choreography.

At nineteen years old, Leo progressed to "director of dance" for his community group and it was this experience that nurtured his "solidarity with dancers." Leo explained that his support was never for "the people who were in charge of me" as his experience as a leader taught him how to become "close to the dancers, in terms of wanting the best for them, wanting to protect them, wanting to make sure that they got the best of everything." As Leo progressed as a dancer, his journey through the dance world led him away from his community group on to joining other dance companies and to study with teachers of different dance forms including ballet, jazz, and contemporary styles.

A long series of dance workshops and performance opportunities led to "working with people at The Repertory Dance Company" and earned Leo the leader's "commitment" to developing his talent. The artist/teacher also recollected the contribution of all the teachers at the Federation School of Dancing, his former teachers from the community arts organizations like Mr. Felix, and "all the people who gave to dance and [contributed their] support whether they were dancers or not." Leo considered them all a part of his evolution to the position that he holds as an associate professor in a college for the arts at Third World School.

When Leo left his native island in the Caribbean, he did so on a scholarship that was created by supporters of the arts. The scholarship took him to the Premier Arts School in New York, where he earned a diploma in dance. Carlton, one of the dancers who Leo considers a close friend, and who now considers himself a "brother" of Leo's, was a student at the school when Leo was completing his studies there. Carlton remembered that "coming to [Premier Arts School] was a very important thing for [Leo] to do and that is where he was able to focus a bit of his training." Carlton also remembered "seeing him in two pieces, two [famous] pieces, . . . one was called 'There is a Time,' and there was another one, . . . it might have been called 'The Traitor'." What is clear to Carlton after all these years is that Leo looked "like a mature, experienced, and powerful performer" early on in his career at the performing arts school. The dance teacher also believed that it was obvious that Leo was more advanced than the other students who were also performing in those presentations at the performing arts school.

Miss Williams, formerly a teacher of Leo and a highly respected dancer in the New York dance circles, also remembered her first encounter with Leo at the Premier Arts School. She was "setting one of [Mr. Leigh's] pieces on the students . . . [and remembered being] only a small part of the learning process" at that point of Leo's education in the arts. She recollected meeting "this very, very tall elegant young man" who was cast in the piece that she had to rehearse with the students. To this day she says that Leo's "silhouette just stands out in my mind" when she recalled his "stature and elegance" and she is convinced that "it wasn't just his height, it was the persona" that made that lasting impression on her. Miss Williams also recalled that many dance companies were courting Leo while he was completing his studies at Premier Arts School. She was certain that Mr. Leigh and the LaSucre companies were two of the outstanding dance entities that were interested in Leo because of his stage presence and maturity, and the fact that he was physically "head and shoulders tall above everyone else."

Miss Banks, another leading figure in the dance world among performers of reputable dance companies, also met Leo when he was a student at Premier Arts School. She also recollected being at the school when "resetting a piece for [Mr.] Donald . . . and . . . [that she] cast Leo in one of the roles" for that dance. She became "interested in him" as a result of a connection that she had with "someone from [Leo's birthplace] that I thought was a very wonderful, instrumental person" in getting "young [Caribbean island] students" to the USA so they could continue their dance training. Miss Banks remembers that Leo "was someone I was drawn to" and that she decided that she was "going to watch him" as he developed his career. She explained that it was her habit to tell students, "I see you; I'm going to watch you. I'm going to be looking at you." Reminiscing about the career that Leo has enjoyed, Miss Banks considered it a blessing that "by the grace of God" she "had the opportunity" to keep her eyes on Leo and his career for over twenty years.

The close connection that Leo developed with Mr. Leigh, through working with his assistants like Miss Williams and Miss Banks at the Premier Arts School, led to a long term relationship with the Ebony Performing Dance Company's school, teachers, and the students. Leo remembered Mr. Leigh's reminder that "the door is always open" for him to join the Ebony Dance School or the dance company, and the fact that it was Mr. Leigh's dance company that "offered me the first scholarship, free passes to the school." This was how Leo developed a relationship with the Ebony Dance School over twenty-two years. Besides keeping personal ties with Miss Williams and Miss Banks, who were formerly dancers with the Ebony Dance Company, Leo was also invited "to teach there and choreograph" soon after she graduated from Premier Arts School. Leo described the experience of working with the EDS on several levels as a dancer, teacher, choreographer, and supporter of the school and company as "wonderful, wonderful, and wonderful." This makes sense if one considered the esteem in which Miss Banks, a former soloist in a famous dance company based in New York, held Leo as a teacher, choreographer, and dancer. She recollected:

> He was a force to be reckoned with on that stage. He really commanded the stage and would today were he just to jump up and do it. Leo was, I mean all the things I say about Leo as a teacher and choreographer, those same ingredients are certainly a part of his performance career because those are the things that really caught the eye and the soul and the heart of the people that were watching him, teaching him, guiding him. . . . And performing with him.

Ebony Dance Company was what Leo described as "the company of my heart, the company that I wanted to dance with all my life," and yet he did not pursue a position with them once he graduated from the performing arts school. Leo recollected that it was "in my first year at Premier Arts School . . . when [Mr.] Leigh invited me to dance for the company but I told him no because it was more important to get the diploma from the school at that time". Many years later Miss Williams, now a close friend of Leo and a dance company director who hires students trained by Leo, suggested that it was due to his "immigration status" that Leo did not join Mr. Leigh's company, and that it was a situation that was "difficult to circumnavigate." Leo, however, maintained a working relationship with the leaders of the dance company and still visits New York to see the company's shows every year "for the past twenty something years." On one opening night he was invited to sit in the company director's seat, an unheard of honor for a visiting artist by

Leo's understanding of the hierarchy of power among dance company leaders. Leo was also pleased to be present in the VIP lounge after the company's performance when Kofi Annan of the United Nations was visiting. He remembered his feeling that he was "shaking hands and talking with and saying hello to Kofi Annan and we are up in the VIP room chit chatting. And I'm sitting in [Ebony Dance Company's director's] seat" and wondering to himself "well how high can you get" after starting out in a lowly "pig pen" of a community dance center on a small island?

Leo went on to join LaSucre Modern Dance Company after graduating from Premier Arts School. Carlton, his friend and colleague from the Premier Arts School days, explained that it was Leo's "first professional" experience. Leo stayed a short while, working with Mr. Lucien, a former teacher from the Premier Arts School, and was then invited to join the G.M. Dance Company. Miss Williams also remembered that "between time . . . he would teach" at different dance schools in order to sustain himself and keep his hand in the classroom. One of the products that came out of Leo's commitment to students and the preservation of his culture as an artist was the occasion of his assignment to present a Caribbean dance workshop at Mr. Leigh's school in New York. Leo explained that he was "commissioned" the first time and that he has "been doing [a workshop] for many years" in the summer. This tradition has continued to this very day.

The progression from new dancer to the Associate Director of the G.M. Dance Company on tour is not lost on any of Leo's mentors and friends. Miss Williams, a dance director of the Ebony Dance Company 2, stated that she and Leo have "talked about this many times, how he came into the [G.M.] company upon invitation and encouragement from one of the former dancers to just moving up in the ranks." Leo is actually considered by G.M. Company members and supporters, according to Miss Williams, to be "one of the people that they rely on to keep that company together not only choreographically but emotionally and spiritually."

Miss Williams recalled that one of the shows that she witnessed when Leo was a performer stood out in her mind. Leo's section in a commissioned work for the G.M. Company "was the gem of the ballet" created by a highly respected opera director and costumed by a famous New York designer. She claimed that part of the success of the piece was due to Leo's being "so tall you can't miss him on stage, so you can't be that tall and be out there and not do [well], okay, that's a self-awareness he has." She also recalled another experience in which she felt that Leo stood out because what he presented "was really him" when he interpreted the role of a shaman and that "it came to fruition . . . really crystallized with him in that role."

Leo described his association with the G.M. Company and that he "made a very powerful commitment to [the leader of G.M. Company] and she was committed to me when she was there working with me." His continued engagement with the dancers in the company is "based on . . . [the] personal relationship" with the company director and her investment in him as an artist. When Leo was a new member in the company, just one year out of Premier Arts School, he was looked after with close attention by then director, Miss Mentor. He recalled "that every time I came into the studio, she'd be like where is my big man? . . . or the nurses [were sent out] to find me or when [the director] got into the theater if we went to tour as soon as the company came in the nurses" would say that Miss Mentor was looking for me. Leo explained this scenario in terms of the fact that he and Miss Mentor "had an incredibly wonderful relationship" as colleagues, dance professionals, and people who loved theater and the arts. This mutually respectful association led the choreographer to create pieces for Leo during the "first three months in the company." Leo was further honored by the choreographer and company director when he was cast in one of the choreographer's "famous dances" and given other opportunities that some of the older members of the G.M. Company were not enjoying at that time. It was a singular achievement for the young dancer who had already served a short term in one dance company and turned down an invitation to join Mr. Leigh's dancers.

Continued association with the G.M. Company led to other opportunities as Leo moved on with his career as a teacher and choreographer. After leaving the company, the board of trustees hired Leo to be director of the South American tour where Leo was "the only artistic person on the tour responsible" for every aspect of the productions at each site.

He worked "fourteen hour days . . . getting up early, doing interviews, checking on dancers who are well, who are not well, who needs a doctor, . . . talk with them, give them a hug, stay with them for a little while until they know that somebody loves them" and other duties associated with the performance production and schedules. The success of this international tour led to another invitation from the G.M. Company and Leo directed the touring production in Europe one summer. Carlton, Leo's "brother," was excited to witness "another very exciting level for him . . . as an artist" and to see how it helped to develop another level of his expertise.

Leo took the opportunity as a director of the international tours to discuss his plans to work with dancers on the island where he was born with the leaders of the G.M. Company. His dream was to mount one of the famous ballets of the G.M. Company on the students at Federation School of Dance in the place where he was born and trained in classical ballet. So Leo left Germany and traveled to his home in the Caribbean in order to begin work with the dancers at the school where he once learned many of the important lessons that were the foundation of his success as a dancer in the USA and other countries. He always presented this opportunity as a means of showing his gratitude to the leading teacher who was supportive of his efforts to leave the island and continue his dance training in the USA. This mission to bring in new dancers from his home town into the professional fellowship of performers was a direct effect of Leo's desire, according to Miss Williams, to "pass on [the knowledge of the discipline] so that these younger dancers can somehow carry the same movement qualities that were happening when [the director of G.M. Company] was alive."

Further commitments to the G.M. Company and his ambition of passing on the legacy of Miss Mentor led Leo to work on grants that have underwritten the cost of hosting the dance company at the Third World School where he now teaches. Miss Banks, a former dancer with the G.M. Company, understood that Leo was "instrumental" in creating the opportunity for his students to study with the company members when they visited the state and to attend the dance company's performances for the public. In the midst of teaching for the high school and college departments at the Third World School, Miss Williams stated that Leo also noted that he was "choreographing [and teaching at] small various studios outside of [Third World School]," and sometimes he went "to New York to work with the G.M. Company and teach company class and conduct rehearsals . . .[and] also be at the . . . school teaching." All of this activity, reflected Miss Williams, was a true representation of Leo's attitude of "giving your all" in every situation.

Character Traits

All three members of Leo's social network were enthusiastic about describing the character traits that accounted for his success on the personal and professional levels. Whether it was his colleague from Premier Arts School who considered him a "brother," or Miss Williams who referred to the "warm person" and the "sense of humor" along with the "integrity" that is the cornerstone of Leo's "sterling reputation," or Miss Banks talking about the "fire, the interest, the dedication" that Leo brought to his work as a student and a professional teacher, dancer, and choreographer, they all commented from a perspective that reflected the full regard for the person who Leo represented to each interviewee.

What Miss Williams considered a "sign of a great artist" included the fact that Leo sees things in situations, for example, and "can deliver it . . . very clearly and very truthfully." This ability is further enhanced by Leo's willingness to "listen" even if he does not "have all of the answers" when someone brings their problem to his attention and wants some answers so they can make a decision. The dance company director further stated that Leo is one of those people who "whether you have good news, bad news, whatever it is, you have a need to share it with this person." The colleague/mentor remembers one instance when Leo proved his level of friendship by supporting her effort to return a pair of shoes to a store after she had worn them. Of course, she now admits that she took too long to return the pair of shoes and should have done the exchange in a timely way. However, she laughed when she recollected that Leo was the one who took the shoes to the store and did his best to get back the money for the purchase. She was amused when she told this story but she used it to demonstrate the kind of loyalty that Leo demonstrated as "that kind of friend" who is supportive and loyal in trying times.

When Miss Banks, Leo's friend and colleague, talked about Leo as "a very focused, passionate dancer" and his evolution to "that same kind of teacher," she went on to elucidate some of the ways in which she saw Leo grow in his discipline. In her estimation Leo never strayed "away from who he was as a person and . . . as a culture." His being from the Caribbean was always integral to who he was on and off stage. He never tried to deny, mask, or deflect the image of his island heritage. Her reflection on Leo as a perpetual student was revealing. She intimated:

> Well, in many ways Leo is, still, sees himself as a student and I think that is a wonderful attribute in any person's life. He's always seeking, he's always learning. The difference that I see now is that he's more mature. He's more determined to speak the truth without fear. You see what I mean, without fear? He works hard, and I do think, I don't know, but it's . . . my gut feeling that he works hard on releasing himself from the fears, whatever they may be. I don't know his personal fears. That he seems to do the searching, the research, self-research and work research . . . so that he has clarity in what he's doing and what he wants to do also.

The colleague and friend who has known Leo the longest since his arrival in the USA is Carlton. His reflections on the way in which Leo has built his life in this country over more than twenty years revealed some insights about the personal culture that Leo represents. Carlton mentioned the fact that Leo has a "strong personality" and that it would either turn some people off of him or bring them in closer. He himself did not have a problem with Leo because he had grown up with his own Caribbean family and he knew how to handle strong personalities. Carlton further described Leo as "gregarious . . . open, friendly, [and a] welcoming person." Also, this college buddy was deeply impressed by the close relationship that Leo had with his aging mother. His "commitment to his mother" was one of the facets of Leo's intimate reality that inspired Carlton to "deeply respect" his friend. It seemed to Carlton that Leo was one of the few family members who took special care of his mother and he liked that trait in his longtime school friend. Carlton recalled that Leo's mother "is very warm," and that he "enjoy[ed] talking with her" especially since he has admired Leo's "very nurturing" attitude towards her "at this point in his life."

He also referred to Leo's wonderful cooking talent. This was the third person to refer to Leo's skill in the kitchen and the fact that it played a very important role in the way that he cemented his relationships with his friends and close associates. According to the accounts of the friends who talked about Leo, people who share food and a passion for eating good food tend to relate in a very intimate way. Miss Williams stated simply that "we love food, he loves to cook" as she smiled and talked about Leo and his kitchen skills. Carlton recalled that he and Leo were "roommates" when they did international tours with G.M. Dance Company and Leo used to cook in the hotel rooms where they stayed in different cities. The former roommate said that it was difficult "to travel around the world not knowing what you are going to be eating" as a professional dancer in a company. He, however, had no problem while on tour since Leo and he were always "well fed . . . [and] Leo would get a little crock pot and . . . make some beans, some stew, some fish, whatever. It was always healthy and good."

Carlton remembered sharing Thanksgiving Day with Leo and the G.M. Dance Company when they were abroad in Hong Kong. He also recalled the tour that took the company to Japan and the fact that Leo was the one who always prepared a good meal at the end of the day. His friends' small travel stove and miniature cooking utensils did not prevent the chef from turning out a gourmet meal at the hotels where the company stayed. To this day, Carlton emphasized, he has taken the same habit of preparing his own meals when he travels as a dance teacher and choreographer. The habit has ensured that his health is maintained and that he keeps in good spirits as he fondly remembers the person who taught him how to take care of himself while on tour.

Leo is regarded for his stellar qualities as a "dear friend" who "keeps you anchored" and this is represented in the kind of advice and rapport that he has established with close associates and friends from his dance circles. Carlton recalled the experience that he survived when he was let go from Ebony Dance Company 2 early in his professional career.

It was Leo who told him to audition for the G.M. Dance Company and counseled him to wear dark clothes "so that the line and the shape of body will stand out." This good advice from Leo ensured that Carlton "got the job." More important than earning the job at the time, it was the fact that Carlton felt that Leo was always "watching out for him" and there to keep him "anchored" that cemented their friendship.

Just as Miss Banks recalled that Leo was always "just so sage, but also not the type of person who was over lording about their wisdom," Carlton recalled the way in which he came to understand Leo and the way he made his way in the world. He intimated that "while [Leo and I] laughed there was always some type of wisdom in the way Leo would speak about something, whatever the topic. I might be complaining about the ills of the dance world or whatever, and Leo always had a knowledgeable way, informed way, and a spiritually informed way of talking about things or offering advice." It is one of the characteristics that helped Carlton to understand the way in which Leo has maintained a solid relationship with one of his former dance instructors and company director for over twenty years. According to Carlton "that [relationship] speaks as well to me about the . . . merit . . . of Leo's work ethic. That he has had this lengthy working relationship with [his former instructor and dance company director] as well . . . [and] it's a good thing."

Leo's Philosophy

An attempt to understand how this dancer/artist/teacher communicates with his students and creates works of art that are appreciated by his colleagues can be supported by a review of some of his comments on the process that facilitates his work in and outside the classroom. Leo intimated his belief that "within an instant, art can bring people together" across "different cultures, different beliefs," and this was brought home to him when he was on tour as an Associate Director of G.M. Company in South America. He noted the "shock" with which people reacted when he was introduced as the leader of the company, a Black man, in the forefront of an internationally recognized dance company. Such a reaction, he felt, was only the surface of a positive ripple effect that was later exposed when droves of students and supporters came to see the show and attend master classes that G.M. Company presented in the country.

Leo's vast experience as a participant in the dance world is appreciated by his friends, former mentors and teachers, Miss Williams and Miss Banks. They both suggested that the best advice that they could share with students who were fortunate enough to study with Leo was to "listen." Miss Banks explained her understanding that the "student would be prepared at some technical level that I would want them to be ready to take a step in [Leo's] direction." In a similar vein, Miss Williams indicated that she would encourage students to "approach your work with immediacy and with a firm commitment to the movement" so that they could benefit from the instruction that Leo would impart to them. The students "should be able to listen" when Leo gave directions, corrections, or suggestions, according to Miss Banks. In further describing how Leo approached his work in the studio with dancers and students, his colleague and friend Miss Williams added:

> You should be able to take criticism because Leo will not lie to you. He will tell you the truth at every level and you have to be able to take that because it is to your benefit. It's to help you . . . and that's very implicit in what he does you know . . . he's there to help you, that he sees how you can be better so he's there to make . . . you make it better.

While it is clear to others that Leo works from a sense of integrity, he espoused a clear understanding of his worth and the high value that he sees reflected in all those who surround him. He explained that he "would always put the dancers first no matter what because I knew clearly what they go through. I know firsthand, I know their personal stories, I know their personal sacrifices . . . more so than . . . usually the people in charge" of a dance school or dance company. With this intimate knowledge in his possession he approaches teaching and choreographing with the attitude that he is "basically in a war . . . but it's a war that at the end of the day, where we may have broken bones and tendons and ligaments and bruised egos . . . we're not burying innocent women and children and [mourn] young men being sacrificed."

Miss Williams, Leo's friend and colleague, has another way of describing the discipline that is engendered in the working relationship that Leo establishes with company members and his students. She talked about the lasting value of a philosophical outlook on life that is encouraged through the culture of good dance training. Miss Williams theorized:

> We know that the discipline of dance can sometimes make life much easier and much more orderly. . . . If you apply that same discipline, passion, commitment to other areas of your life, you know, It really can help you move forward in life and break down barriers and . . . remove obstacles. . . . it's the thing that helps you survive in life. And whether you become a dancer or whatever you become beyond that point, it's the survival mechanism.

Leo teaches both high school and college students and finds that each group demands "psychological levels that are totally different from each other" and that he has "to be prepared to work with" these two levels every day. At the time that he was interviewed about his first years at the Third World School he had choreographed 14 dances for the school and had a clear philosophical approach to the dancers worked out. Leo explained:

> The dances again are always based on trying to help develop the students to be professional artists, so . . . [I] have to take stuff the way [students] are at that point and [consider] where . . . I think they can go artistically and technically . . . and also to grow as a person as well. So I create the dance that we have along those lines. Not just composed of steps but of some background and interest to them and [connected] to some experience in their lives.

Leo considered this insight into his students' lives invaluable since he has learned that some students are coming from the inner city and that they are sometimes dealing with the challenges of "illiteracy, poverty" and personal issues that are a great source of their strength and distraction. With this knowledge in hand, Leo tries "to bring material to the young students that they can connect with . . . that can help them to make themselves [better] and move forward . . . to use that as a tool to find a way to deal with issues in their lives." The result of his efforts at establishing this rapport is that "it works out quite well" for the students and improves his efficiency at establishing good relations in his exchanges in the classroom early on in the students' dance career.

Through these varied experiences of reaching out to his students, Leo has found that he understands the fact that "perfection of teaching is . . . creating a thing of quality, both for the student and the teacher. Experiencing the quality provides a place where the student does not have an ism of fear, the ism of lack, the ism of limitation" and in that freedom both teacher and student are able to collaborate successfully. Leo also included the awareness necessary for working successfully with a student in regard to learning background knowledge as far as making an effort

> . . . to discover how does that student live, is the student left-brain, right-brain, or does the student learn better through individual [instruction], or through hearing [directions] or will the student learn something faster if you manipulate or [physically] move the student into the shape or will the student learn better if you speak it out or will the student learn better if you are to demonstrate or a mixture of all of that, or if the student will learn better if the student were put [at the] back in the room and sort of left to his own.

One of the highlights of Leo's experience with educating his students in the lore of working in professional dance companies was the exposure that Ebony Dance Company 2 provided to his school. Leo wanted his high school and college students to "realize the connection between the craftsman work that we do in daily [dance] technique classes and how that transfers itself into performance" on stage. When the professional dancers from Ebony Company 2 did "a lecture demonstration . . . technique classes and . . . a performance of their own. . . . the students were very moved, very inspired," and were "able to realize that a lot of what [Leo's] been saying and working with them on a lot [in class and] . . . that it actually works . . . with another dance company."

Leo believes that his students' success, like his, is a result of "phenomenal hard work and discipline and the support of people who respected and honored that hard work and discipline" along the way. He believes that students' "authentic and original source of creativity" must be acknowledged so that they do not feel that teachers have "chopped off their spirituality." This orientation to his young stewards is based on the fact that Leo "only bow[s] to that which is within me and which I know to be [within you] so that [its divine presence] makes us equal."

The Students

Among the many accolades that Leo is proud to discuss is the success of his students in national competitions: two won in the National Advancement for the Arts presentation one year, and on the stage as professional performers with famous dance companies. He was also happy to report that "one of my students who I also teach at a private school . . . made it into the Premier Arts School." He has trained students at the high school and college levels and introduced them to the leaders at Ebony Dance Company and G.M. Company over many years. He has also been able to see his students graduate from Third World School and go into the studios directed by Ebony Dance School and G.M. Dance School. Miss Williams described one of the graduates of Leo's training at Third World School as "a very tall, very beautiful young man . . . and that young man is extraordinary." The director of the Ebony Dance Company 2 also recollected that:

> I know this summer there were two or three [students] that were up here [at Ebony Dance School] on scholarship that . . . I had the privilege of teaching while Leo was away. Everybody [at the EDS] was in love with them because they were so focused and so ready and serious and when they went to class they just took all of their discipline, that directness, that focus that they had learned from Leo, right to the class. So, they were never placed in a lower level class it was always THE advanced [classes].

Miss Banks spoke in the same vein and talked about Leo's students in terms of their high level of "preparedness" and the fact that they are "eager and hungry to learn, to go further. They're very polite and respectful. They work hard, they're disciplined . . . very talented people."

When Carlton reflected on Leo's decision to move to the southern state where he now teaches at Third World School, he said that Leo "made a good move, he was able to finish another degree" while he was teaching and choreographing for other dance companies and traveling to different states. Both Carlton and Miss Williams have witnessed Leo's "strong impact on the students" at Third World School and they have seen and met "very strong confident dancers" who have studied or auditioned at two schools in New York after graduating from their former school.

Leo's sense of accomplishment and pride are the result of the hard work and deep commitment that he has made to his students. This attitude was reflected in his tone when he reminisced about seeing three of his former students performing in New York with the Ebony Dance Company. Leo enthused: "Two of [of those former students] I actually took by their hands and brought them into the Ebony Dance School . . . and then the director took them into the [first] company. And now they're up [on stage in New York] they're stars, dancing in the [famous] company."

How does Leo accomplish these goals with his students? Miss Williams attested to the fact that Leo's students feel that they have "someone who has been very key in their life, who has been very encouraging . . . he is admired . . .100%." Carlton, who has been a close friend of Leo since their early dance school days, stated that Leo is "doing some really strong work . . . especially for minority or underserved minority communities or [the] underserved student population." Miss Williams has also observed that Leo

> . . . is very serious about his responsibilities in transferring movement and transferring choreography [to dancers]. He not only gives you the steps, he gives you the why of the steps. The meaning of the steps. And what your body should do with this movement. What your body must make of this movement and what your spirit and mind must make of this movement [that is taught in class].

Leo understands that he is there to "help to develop their talents so they are ready and prepared to go not only to Third World School but beyond." He has seen students mature into dancers who audition for Premier Arts School in New York and the dance schools attached to Ebony Dance Company, New York 2 Dance Company, and the G.M. Dance Company. The famous dance companies all operate out of New York City and travel across the globe when they are on tour outside the USA.

Making connections with the students

It isn't difficult to understand how Leo builds the rapport with his students when you listen to his process for developing choreography and staging his pieces. In his description of the way in which he hones in

on the qualities that individual dancers are directed and rehearsed, he
explained his methodology in this way:

> First of all I am looking for particular strengths [in the dancer], when it has
> to do with competitive dancing, it's competition . . . [I have to decide] are
> they much more athletic, are they much more dramatic. . . . Even though they
> may have potential in those same areas whether dramatic or athletic, I choose
> the solos based on which one . . . I feel [would] do best in terms of those two
> concepts.

Leo described his experience with one male dancer who began his
formal dance training at Third World School just 14 months before he
was cast in a major role that Leo created for him. Leo explained that he
does not "speak to human time." The teacher/artist outlined his process
for creating work that this student could handle with artistic sensibility,
based on the fact that the student knew "how to transfer dramatic information into dance movement and to do it so quickly and so clearly and
so vibrant[ly] and with so much passion." Leo was convinced, based
on this experience, that his teaching method "speaks to the naturalness
of intelligence . . . that's accessible to every single human being on the
planet." This student was chosen to portray the character Nijinsky as a
persona representing his private thoughts. Leo "knew that this [student]
would be someone that I would be able to do incredible things with [in
the choreography]" due to his "instinct to move naturally." The choreographer's hunch about the student's ability to handle the advanced
dance assignment as "Nijinsky speaking in his mind and him dancing
the words itself . . . worked out brilliantly." According to Leo's theory
of teaching youth, he was right about the fact that: "Divine intelligence
knows nothing about time so I can go straight to [the student] and speak
to him directly as communicating with divine intelligence and divine
intelligence will respond."

The Teaching Philosophy

There is an evolution in Leo's decision to take on the task of becoming
a successful teacher. He remembered making the decision, after accom-
plishing many feats as a performer, that "the next thing in my life was

teaching," and asking himself "Now what would that be, the perfect teacher or the perfection of teaching?" This led him to accept the invitation from Third World School to be a faculty member and to create dances for high school and college students. Leo believes, after creating 14 new dance pieces and mentoring hundreds of students into the profession of dance performance, that he has "arrived at the place where I can teach almost flawlessly." His confidence as a teacher has not been achieved easily and his mentors and friends have been witnesses to his evolution in the classroom. Miss Williams, director of Ebony Dance Company 2, has had the opportunity to see Leo share his understanding about "the whole lifestyle of dance and artist" with his students and young company members. She also has observed that "he is such a nurturer of dancers at every level. And dancers love him. I'm sure that when he talks to them each individual feels that they are the only ones in the room." In her estimation, it is an "amazing thing to watch him transfer . . . not just information about movement but about the drama of movement, and the drama of life" when he is teaching in a professional dance company or at the Third World School.

Leo made his approach to teaching clear when he described the benefits of students learning technique, whether it is in the form of ballet, Martha Graham movement, or Caribbean folk dance. He explained that "technique helps to make things clearer, but you do not need a whole lot of technique from the beginning to be able to express that intelligence that is natural in the world." In his experience as a dancer and teacher of dancers he has realized that "the intelligence is there. It is always there, it's in you . . . if you have a body that has the strength and a certain amount of training and technique to do it." Of course, technique is a foundation that allows talent to express itself.

When he teaches Martha Graham technique he uses his understanding of the process based on his work with his teachers, what he learned when dances were choreographed for him, and the information that he gathered as he "learned to dance." Through many years of study and performance, Leo "understood why a movement was done this way was because it was telling me this particular thing and this particular story." Miss Williams, who once studied the Martha Graham technique, witnessed this attitude to the movements and their use in Leo's choreography. She described

Leo as going "to the depth" when he taught a "Graham ballet or an Afro-Caribbean ballet and ballets of his creation." She also came to believe that Leo's approach to the dancers gave "them this coat or cloak that will sustain them through so many things in life, it's just amazing." As far as she could tell, Leo became a "parent" figure to many students.

This "going to the depth" that Miss Williams has witnessed in Leo's approach to his collaboration with dancers may be explained by the teacher's belief that he always addresses "the spirituality" of the individual being. He has learned that in speaking with students any mention of spirituality is confused with religion, and that the "mention of divinity is the mention of God and God in the context of the Judeo-Christian sense or the Father sense which includes the Muslims and so on and so forth and their tradition," but this is not what he addresses in his students. Leo encourages his students to go to another level of understanding of their divine nature, the essence of their being, and how it expresses itself in the world.

Leo has limitations on the time and content of the interactions with his dancers. He mentioned that they "do not work everyday and we do not have the time and space" to do a lot of small group work. Leo further explained:

> The only time I ever, ever see all the dancers is the night of the first performance for the entire year. . . . Kids have to leave to go home or [they have to meet] their parents or they're sick, or this or that. So not even in the [dress rehearsal] sometimes I get to see all the people and by that time it's too late anyway to do anything [more than tidy up the choreography and make sure that people feel secure with entrances and exits].

When he was able to bring in guest teachers from famous dance companies, including Ebony Dance Company, G.M. Dance Company, or Fanon Dance Company, the students "learned a lot and [were] able to realize that a lot of what [Leo was] saying and working with them on a lot, that it actually works," because they were able "to actually see [the dance technique application] happen with another dance company." Miss Banks, a former dancer with G.M. Company, recollected that Leo "brought me down to teach, and other people that I guess he trusts and wants the children to be exposed to," since Leo believes that "they'll need in their beginning stages as students to see other [dancers teach class and then direct performances]."

Leo has also developed an understanding that he described as the need for the teacher to know

> . . . some background, some information about the students' lives, where they live, [about]the parents, [who] the siblings are, perhaps even to some degree, what is the financial situation of that household of that student . . . does the student suffer abuse? These are the kinds of things that you look for because students respond to that [understanding from the teacher].

He was always careful to observe if "maybe a loud voice" can "intimidate" a student, and whether "certain topics . . . are talked about and in what context those topics are [discussed]." For example, "typical jokes" for one group of students have been observed to "cause a student to shut down and stop learning." All of these aspects of the students' behavior are taken into consideration as Leo comes to understand "where that person needs to be in order for that person to start learning" in the dance classroom.

When Miss Banks described the "very wonderful journey" of Leo as a choreographer, she referred to the fact that "his choreography just mature[d] and take[n] on content . . . with such imagination." Miss Williams, the dance company director, gave an example of Leo's "general creativity with movement" when she mentioned her experience of him casting a large number of dance students in an end of semester presentation at Ebony Dance School. She stated that:

> Somehow he does [the casting of every student in the class]. And everybody has something to do . . . he brings the costumes for them to perform in, you know . . . everything they need he brings with him [from Third World School or his personal collection]. He goes and has the music mixed, and . . . that's several hours [of work] right there to get it right . . . to go to a sound engineer and put all that together.

This statement is made with a sense of awe since it is atypical of the kind of investment that teachers make when they are in a school setting and not a professional dance company context.

Leo described his journey with one set of students and their original choreography as a move to eliminate "the one artist . . . idea." He asked the students to submit their ideas for a dance piece and then decided that he would not tell anyone if "it was their material I was using." When Leo began creating movement, he "created a dance that would fit that particular temperament and the mind temperament" of the dancer who was given the opportunity to portray the story or the theme that a student had submitted for consideration. Leo's approach to each student was based on the idea that he should "try to challenge them by giving them something opposite from what seems to be natural for them to do" as far as an athletic or a dramatic quality of their physical expression.

Leo was careful to direct the students so that they didn't "bring in . . . any preconceived ideas of what [the dance] should be" and he also avoided any "vibes that might not have been positive for them working . . . [in the] place if students found that somebody's work was chosen over their work." The result of this sensitive and creative approach to making the students the center of the collaborative process led to a successful production that was well-received by other students, parents, mentors, and dance faculty. Leo elaborated on his creative process as a director of the students when he described his journey to the opening night of the performance. He explained:

> So I sort of kept [the original student story] in the dark and then I would throw out general ideas based on the information that I had and then had the person who wrote the story start coming up with material based on sort of an abstract image and concepts on their own work. . . . Or I would have somebody else who I felt might be able to bring certain qualities or information to that concept [bring in dance movement and images]. And I started working on it like that and finally it all started to come together but it actually took quite awhile to put the dance [together] over the year, it took the longest time to come together.

He was convinced from the start of the collaboration with the students, however, that he "didn't want to interfere too much with what they were bringing" and that his job was simply "to more or less guide" their expression in movement. And the result was that "some very interesting things came out of it" and both the students and Leo learned important lessons from the creative process.

In Leo's considered opinion, such trust-building exercises as the collaboration in choreography is at the basis of his witnessing so many of the students succeed at the National Dance Competition and go on to earn scholarships at leading arts organizations including Premier Arts School, Ebony Dance School, Ebony Dance Company 2, and G.M. Dance School. Looking back on his journey with his students from high school, through college, to the professional dance schools in major cities, Leo recalled that one of his proudest moments was the realization that three of his former students were company members of the G.M. Dance Company when he was associate director and rehearsal director of the South American tour.

Signs of the Times

As with his own performance experience, Leo works with his college and high school students to ensure that they can eventually say about their performance of choreography that "the dance is happening because I work so hard, so many long hours, even when I'm sleeping I'm working. And so that I never have to be distracted by the choreography," at the end of all their rehearsals. One competition in which his students have performed has over 4,000 students, some of the best young artists from throughout the entire country, and Leo explains that "several of my students have won first place and have been awarded presidential scholarship appointments from that program."

In the pursuit of appropriate dance selections for the individual students, Leo has trained himself to be a connoisseur of music and student tastes in musical styles. The experienced choreographer explained his relationship to music and how it has affected his creativity as a performing artist and teacher. As far as he could analyze his response to music he had this understanding that if

> . . . you play music . . . something happens to me and I can transform myself into states of mind. What it looks like physically, I don't know. What effect it has, I'm not too sure. But I know personally the actual connection that I have with music . . . and the force that is me or the God force or the creed, whatever you want to call it, is one and the same. So therefore when I hear music, it's an experience in ability on a higher level. And then my being starts to express itself on a certain level, which people call dance, but for me I'm not dancing, I'm having an experience.

This connection to music and its expression in his creative work is represented by the wide range of styles that he chooses for his dancers. He has used music from as wide a selection as Ella Andell of Trinidad, Mercedes Sosa of Argentina, and John Coltrane of the USA. He has also worked with European classical music in his creation about the famous Russian dancer, Nijinsky, and the music score for "Frida" in another production for the high school students.

The "experience" that Leo describes, in his interpretation of music as he knows it, allows him to connect to dance movement as it appears in different continents across the globe. His decision to use "crumping," a dance form that has been documented in South Los Angeles, has led him to research that shows the same movement expression appearing in Africa, in places like the Sudan. Leo explained his understanding of the connection of the two movement styles as "The same structure, the same construction, the same body temperament . . . and you're talking about dances thousands of years old [that reappear in the USA in modern times]." This insight into the historical context of dance movement explained the choice of crumping for a dance sequence that Leo developed in collaboration with his students to express a generational response to the present challenges of society. Leo used "the same dramatic expression—psychological and physical" to demonstrate how

> . . . the same thing that happened in the sixties [in this country] is more or less the same [social response to crises] that's happening in 2006 and therefore . . . that contemporary dance movement that came out from the sixties . . . [blended] with the crumping movement that's coming out from the inner-cities in the 2000s.

Further efforts by Leo to identify with the experience of the dancers at the high school and college levels comes from an understanding that many of the students have tremendous personal challenges that they work to overcome. Leo recollected that:

> One [student's] . . . father was murdered in prison last summer and another one lost both his parents to AIDS, . . . there's [sic] several of them who are fatherless or motherless or both parents are gone. . . . Their parents are not around, they either died from drug overdoses, AIDS, murder, or they're in prison and they'll be adopted by grandparents or [the young men are] bringing themselves up.

This sensitivity to his students' emotional experiences, particularly the young Black male dancers, led Leo to find ideas that could connect with the background experiences that some of the students represented. The choreographer's desire to put the knowledge and skills that he had developed during his performing and directing tenure at the G.M. Company, for example, the "use of music and the phenomenal musicians and composers and the set design . . . and the costume design and the phenomenal dancing by some of the best contemporary dancers in the world," made him aware that he could harness "the creative aspects of . . . the costumes, the lights, and the music and the scene [design]" to tell the diverse stories of the youth in his dance programs.

When the dancer/artist decided to include "the voices of the dancers themselves," with "their own stories" rather than the choreographer's vision, he turned to their classroom experience in writing to get them on the track of thinking like creators. In the process of developing movement that expressed the emotions embedded in the stories, the students were invited to

> . . . write some poetry or stories, [or about] some experience in their life that was very important to them, that was very intense, perhaps traumatic . . . it meant a lot to them, [had] a lasting effect of change or some sort of transformation for them and so they all wrote stories and brought [them] in.

The result was that the students shared experiences of transformation, in Leo's estimation, that explored "extremely tragic and violent" and "really emotional stuff." There were poems and stories and Leo decided to "take some of that material . . . the ones that I felt . . . would be chorographical [easy to translate into movement symbols] if that's a word."

The dance suite began with a "group theme" accompanied by music from a female artist from Trinidad. The lyrics, by Azell, asked questions about what was happening with the children in society, talked about them being "left behind and not being [looked] after" by adults and society. This evolved into a section about homelessness and one character represented the plight of women who have been looked over and discarded by society. Leo shared a description of a costume that was designed for one of the lead dancers that included:

> Torn up clothes and at the last second, a few days before the concert, I put
> paper bags in her hair, attached plastic bottles and tin cans all over the costume
> . . . so that it made its own noise while she was moving across the floor.

The student represented an emotion that was first articulated in a piece of writing that was prompted by a significant life experience and then interpreted in response to music.

Nijinsky as a Muse

One of the highlights of Leo's time with the Third World School is the production of the dance based on Nijinsky, the famous Russian dancer. The choice of this subject from Leo's perspective could be understood in reference to the fact that

> . . . Nijinsky suffered . . . because he had to leave his family that he was so close
> to and . . . went through a lot of hardship and . . . had to find his way through
> [bourgeois society] . . . and turned out to be one of the great geniuses of the
> dance of the 20th century.

Leo felt that his young male dancers could identify with the 12-year-old boy who got into one of Russia's premier dance schools and struggled to make a name for himself while his family endured poverty and separation from him. The young male dancers under Leo's supervision could also understand the heavy burden of being the one in the family who was identified as the "winner" because he won a place at a prestigious art school and was carded to be the single success that the family could identify in their whole history.

In fact, Leo recalled that one of his young dancers came from "a family that did not have a whole lot [financially]" and that "they did not have any money and their family was depending . . . [and hoping that] he would get into the school of the arts and make it." Leo was not daunted by the fact that the ballet required "so much breadth in terms of the use of the imagination and character building" and was amply repaid for his patience and faith in the students' ability to communicate the story at the end of the rehearsal process. He was able to witness the skill with which his young dancers grew into the characters that they represented in Nijinsky's life and how they learned to be "confident . . .

as young artists [who] . . . understand the craft [of dance performance] to practice in it."

The choice to do an expanded version of the ballet was based on Leo's concern that the relationships in Nijinsky's life would be better represented by the college students. The choreographer wanted to "involve . . . Nijinsky's relationship with Diaghilev [his mentor and director at the dance company] which was a homosexual one" as well as the relationship Nijinsky had with his wife. Leo was aware that the dancers had to represent "psychological states that contributed perhaps to his [clinical] madness" and that the college dancers would be able to interpret "the larger story" with "the madness and the hatred and the rage of all the different things that ha[d] happened to [Nijinsky] in his life." The mature students would also have to consider the impact on Nijinsky of "the loss of his father, the moving of the family [from one town to another], the betrayals that happened to him between his lovers [male and female], [and] his [difficult relationship with] his wife." The process of getting the dancers to represent these psychological states, as interpreted by Leo, was a "slow" one, and it did take the young college artists on a journey to "very intense mature, dark" emotional aspects of the life of Nijinsky.

While the creative process was involved and required skill on both the parts of teacher and students, Leo realized that as a teacher it was "best to just . . . give a general overview [of the story of Nijinsky's life] and then leave [the dancers] alone." His idea was to first get the dancers comfortable with the steps and then to move slowly into the "deeper, dark, psychological colorings or emotional states [that the characters represented] for them to work on." The teacher/artist felt that he was "feeding" or "nursing" the dancers so that they could handle a little bit of material at a time and "as they start to get comfortable" then "bring more of the deeper information, dark information about the experiences that Nijinsky had," so that the dramatic storyline could unfold in the movements.

Leo, as a seasoned performer and teacher, understood that it was important not to let the dancers become "overwhelmed at the beginning and [therefore] run away from [the material], or give up," before they explored the full emotional states of the characters. He was convinced that if he paid attention to the cues from the dancers that he would not "give them more [than] they ask[ed] for" during the rehearsals of the piece.

Leo's Legacy

There are many ways in which one can talk about the impact of Leo's tenure in the lives of the young dancers who he mentors and instructs in dance and life lessons. Those friends and colleagues who have had a long time to observe and experience his career on and off stage, in classrooms, and other social events, have had a lot of grist for their reflections. Comments from his mentors, colleagues, and former roommate help to provide a lens through which we can assess some of the facets that go into the success of his career as a teacher and choreographer.

Miss Williams and Miss Banks, one a dance company director, the other a dancer who teaches and rehearses dance companies, wish that all the good that Leo has put into the world "comes back around." As the person who "has the information and shares the information with clarity and truth and passion and dedication," it is obvious that he has built a loyal following among some of the most esteemed dance practitioners in this country. Further, when Carlton talks about Leo's rise to a respected choreographer and artistic director for the touring company of G.M. Company, he says so with pride and the full knowledge that his place at Third World School "has really made a tremendous difference in what those students are getting, especially . . . being a black man, an African American, a Caribbean [person]." Leo's former roommate is also aware that Leo's presence among the young people at the dance schools is an important experience in the lives of some of the children "who may not be quite as advantaged as far [as] having entrée into certain areas" in education sites.

Miss Banks, who has taught classes for Leo at Third World School, recollected "many positive things for how Leo affects other people's lives." She not only remembered the way he has "taken the things he has received" and used them to "enrich other people," including his feeding of people and the "nurturing thing" that he shows in the encouragement of their careers and personal dreams. But she was aware that Leo gives his students "a certain exposure, a certain direction that is serious, that has some historical attachment and background," and that would be one of his lasting effects on his young charges at New World School, Ebony Dance School, and G.M. Dance Company's studio.

Gerard

Light
Faster than
Sound
Movement   Bigger
Than eyes   Blinking
Shutters that come   And go
And see and   Document
And   Transform to
Images

The screen
On which
Life
Is /Projected
Heart   That hears
The beats   Of
Hope   Dreams
Imagination
Filter   Lens   Points of
Clarity   So obvious   Clean   Unflinching
But only to   Those
Who   Choose   Light.

Chapter Four

Gerard's Gift

Gerard could be described as a global citizen because he travels a great deal and does his lighting design work in theaters as far-flung from his home island as Brazil, Spain, Vancouver, and the USA. He suggested that his ability to adapt to different cultures and the demands of various skin tones under lights and temperatures on stage came from his education in his native land. The designer explained that students in his country "know about people in China from the time we're quite small," for example, and that was probably why they "have a different perspective, it's a much broader perspective" on the world and the people who live in it than those students and faculty that he met when he was training in the USA. The fact that his upbringing brought this understanding to him early in life assured him that he could "embrace a wider scope of stuff" in the theater environment and made it possible for him to work with people from different backgrounds and "embrace different cultures."

As early as high school, when one of his classmates encouraged him to go to a popular local theater and get involved in the dramatic production that was being mounted, Gerard was attracted to the work of managing the actors and musicians who worked on the play. This first experience at a semi-professional theater near his secondary school led him to meeting some of the leading artists in his native country. These included the principal of a dance school that sent students to the Alvin Ailey American Dance Theater; the drama workshop members that trained actors for companies in Canada, London, and the USA; and the leaders of a television production workshop that would evolve into a national television production house. The young apprentice stage manager then went on to work on several productions with one successful playwright and was called on by other performing companies to bring his skills in lighting design and stage management to their presentations.

Gerard admitted that he would not "have had that initiative on my own in those days" to go to the theaters where he was first known as a regular supporter and skilled craftsman. The master lighting designer remembered clearly that "any person training in [that country] or working in theaters has got to be multi-faceted" and the person had to "still sort of help . . . set lights up or . . . [learn the skill of] calling cues" so that all the technical jobs backstage were filled. Mixing with the other technicians in different areas of stage production led to Gerard's interest in "lighting . . . scenery, sound, costuming" and later on production management. Much later on in his career on the island he was introduced to making masks and building costumes with a band of masqueraders who would become the producers of an opening show for one of the Olympics presentations in another country.

A strong work ethic and commitment to the development of the national theater scene led Gerard to being able to do the research that helped him understand that "nobody has a bachelor's, let alone master's degree in lighting from the Caribbean but myself." This status of formal training came about through his work on plays with a resident playwright on his home island. The playwright was doing a term of teaching in an English department in another country during the days that Gerard was still keeping a day job and doing his theater work in the evenings in his home country. The lighting designer explained that it was a time when there was "a whole bunch of us that [the playwright] had coached to come out somewhere to get training." The idea was to get young people professionally trained so that they could come back to the island and help to improve the standards of production at all the theaters. After much soul searching, and raising the exorbitant funds to pay for his first degree abroad, Gerard made up his mind to quit the island and move to the USA to earn his first degree.

The Master designer recalled that he was "tinkering" with lighting design "back then" when he was a student at Theater University. These were "exciting times" as Gerard recalled the days when he was the sole technical student representing the theater scene from his country in a foreign prestigious theater program. After he attained his first degree at that school, while working with the same playwright who first encouraged him to pursue his dream as a professional technician, he decided to head to New York and start working as a hired hand for productions. A few years into that stint in the big city led Gerard back to his native land where he fortunately found work in a new theater that seated 400 people and had state of the art lighting equipment. This theater was the first of its kind in the country, and Gerard was the first person to have a full time job as its resident lighting designer and manager.

A longtime friend and production manager remembered meeting Gerard more than twenty years ago when he invited her and her company to stage their production at the new theater in their home city. As the veteran producer talked about her history with Gerard, it became clear that this introduction to the theater and the savvy director who could make her plays look good was the beginning of a long and successful relationship.

Janice, the theatrical producer, explained that Gerard was the first person who she had worked with on the island who was not just interested in "turning the lights on and off" on the stage. Having served as a vice president of a drama association and the director of her own theater company, Janice was in a good position to judge the merits of Gerard soon after he returned from his stint at Theater University in the USA. She recalled that Gerard was the technical director of the new facility in the capital city and that he was "one of the few people who was interested in design" in the country. Very few people even had the opportunity to do theater production on a full time basis and Gerard was managing up to 30 plays at the theater every year. Janice recounted that Gerard thought that "the amount of seats in the auditorium was perfect for theatre" and he enjoyed the fact that for the first time in the island's history "actors were employed regularly for the nine or ten years" that he was there as the leader of that production team.

The time came, however, when Gerard felt it was time to "go back and get my master's" so that he could do a wider range of jobs behind the scenes at the theater. Referring to his excellent networking skills, he explained that he met someone at a conference where he was presenting a paper on Caribbean theater design and she insisted that he join her as a student at the Institute of Theater in the USA (a fictional name). It was hard to give up a full time job as a manager and resident designer of his country's newest facility and go back to school, Gerard admitted. But the young manager plucked up his courage and jumped into the fray of being a student and a teaching assistant at the theater training program in the USA.

Two years out of the training program at the Institute of Theater, with a lot of experience from working on shows as a guest designer for various productions while he was a master's student, he joined the teaching faculty at the Institute of Theater. As an assistant professor he taught courses in lighting design and insisted on taking his talented students out on the road to work alongside him as he mounted his designs and supervised productions in professional theaters. He was invited to show his designs at Southern University at one point and this led to an invitation to work at the campus while they were building the graduate theater program. Gerard reminisced about his time on that campus in the southern USA and the fact that the program "had been quite undeveloped." His response to that situation was to say "this is a good challenge" and he stayed on as an assistant professor at the campus for one year.

Hanna remembered that Gerard was "a breath of fresh air" on the campus when she was the chair of the department at Southern University. He was quite a curiosity to the students who were intrigued by the fact that Gerard was "a person of color who spoke with a British accent." Gerard's professional and wide experience, coupled with his genuine interest in developing student talent, led to him being a favorite among the people he taught. Hanna remembered that Gerard "developed quite a following" among the students and that he always involved them in his professional assignments.

As a specialist in jazz dance and modern dance movement, Hanna was deeply appreciative of the wide perspective on world theater that Gerard brought to the students. The former department chair whose teaching responsibilities included "ballet technique and choreography

. . . dance history and . . . dance and world culture" also explained that Gerard "would teach courses in lighting design . . . design for the . . . dance productions and the theater productions" and that he "served on committees" within the theater department. During Gerard's time at Southern University as "the lighting designer in [the school's] department of dance and theater," he created designs for two of the productions that Hanna mounted for her dance students. These experiences allowed Hanna and Gerard "to work creatively together" and develop a strong bond during his short tenure at the institution.

But then the call came from the Institute of Theater again and Gerard chose to help the institution develop their offering beyond an "established bachelor program" for novice designers. At this point in his career, he settled into the teaching regime in academia for three solid years. Gerard was at the school when "we had the horrible thing happen on the campus, which kind of rocked everybody's world and turned things around" for students, faculty, and staff. The safety of all the people who were part of the campus was seriously challenged through an unfortunate incident of violence. Gerard talked about "the Valentine's Day that you will never forget" and trembled at the thought of the danger that people had to face from the threat of one student's actions. Yet, Gerard remembered his time at Institute of Theater as one when he accumulated "a couple of awards and nominations for very prestigious things" in professional theater. He admitted "that was really very exciting" and it gave him the confidence to keep pushing for more professional standards in his class offerings and from his graduate and undergraduate students.

The Light in the Tunnel

Three close colleagues, also considered Gerard's friends, found it easy to talk about the character traits that endeared him to each of them. Janice, from his native land, remembered meeting Gerard at least twenty years ago when she was at the start of her career in theater production. To this day, she thinks about the meeting with this gifted lighting designer and production manager as one of the most important moments in her career. She talked about his demeanor during the mounting of a production as "calm" and basically supportive of the actors and her production team by meeting their demands and constantly saying that "everything is fine if that's what you want" when he worked to meet the expectations of the director. Janice explained that the idea that things have to go "my way and it has to be this way [or no way]" is never associated with Gerard's process during production. Because his results are always outstanding, Janice always approaches working with him with the faith that she can "trust exactly what he will do" to turn out well. Gerard's actions have always shown that the production team "is in this together," and therefore he puts in his full effort to make everything excel.

Two colleagues who worked with Gerard at Southern College for one year reminisced about his "presence" and the "caring" attitude that he expressed with students. Nikki, a dance professor at the university, particularly enthused about the fact that Gerard was an artist on and off campus. She commented that he was "just a wonderful breath of fresh air here in our department because his perspective is so broad," in comparison to some colleagues who divorce themselves from one side of the profession or the other to meet their needs as theater practitioners. She recalled that his "broad perspective" and cultural experiences from across the world enlivened the creative work that was done during the year that he was a lighting designer on their campus. The professor of dance also recalled that she felt very comfortable telling Gerard if she "did not like" a design idea or a lighting plan that he selected for her dance pieces. He would adjust his plans to try and meet her creative expectations so that the production reflected her ideals.

The idea that the lighting designer "was well bred" always came through in the way that he showed "respect" to all who worked with him at Southern University. His friend and colleague, Nikki, who worked closely with Gerard on several dance productions also observed that the artist was "more interested in getting people to think and communicate" and would support people "taking a nature walk" to enhance their creative output when they felt challenged to produce under severe scheduling demands. He was deeply appreciated by his colleagues in the department because he was always "professional" in his work on and off stage and in performing the academic service that was part of his job description. Comparing the effect of Gerard on her to a famous musician, Nikki described the experience of seeing and hearing Miles Davis play during the last months of his life.

The professor of dance said that Miles Davis was just "magic" to see as he worked at that level of performance. And then when Davis died soon after that show she realized that he was gone for good. She felt that Gerard had the same effect on the students and faculty on Southern University's campus when he "worked his magic" and then left their institution for his next post. Nikki admitted that she did not only miss Gerard because of his "creative spirit" but because he, too, was a person of color. She realized after his departure from the school that she did not have that kind of camaraderie, as a person of color, with any other colleague up to, or after, the time that Gerard joined the faculty as a lighting designer.

Hanna believed that Gerard "just has the type of work ethic, that also people respond to and students wanted to emulate" in order to be successful. The professor, who taught dance and a course on world cultures, was deeply impressed by the kind of attention that Gerard paid to each production. Describing herself as someone who is "not creative," she related her experience when Gerard encouraged her to complete a choreographic work that had always been on her mind but never seemed to move on to a production for others to see. Hanna admitted that "choreographically speaking" she credits Gerard for supporting her as she "took another step in my own craft" when he engaged her in a creative brainstorming process.

Gerard listened to her ideas and then "he sent me this beautiful sketch of a costume, it was wonderful. I was just stunned the he took the time to do that for me." The costumes were ones that Gerard imagined the dance piece would need if they mounted the production with the college students. This act of generosity touched Hanna deeply and made her realize that Gerard's ability to give his full attention to each person who was asking for his creative input was a rare quality among peers on the campus and beyond that academic site. The choreographer explained: "you know how some people have creative temperament, I never experienced that with [Gerard]. So he has a foot in both worlds, in academia and in the professional world, and he's able to bring those professional experiences into academia to enrich the program."

In each of the three recollections by these female associates and friends, Gerard was described with warm affection. The fact that he traveled widely and did productions in many countries and states in the USA made him a person whose opinions and values on aesthetics for the theater were deeply appreciated. Nikki, the dance professor, recalled showing Gerard three masks that a friend had given her as a gift and how he immediately started talking about the origin of the masks and explained that "the hands come together, this is a water spirit and it is diving" and encouraged her to hang it up from the other end so that it could look like it was entering the water. Nikki was amazed that Gerard knew the origin of the African masks and that he was so at ease when he explained their significance to her on the spur of the moment.

Janice, the colleague from Gerard's native island, talked about "trust" in Gerard and the "extremely valuable" impact that the designer had on her "work or my life." The theater producer emphasized the fact that "there was no one else . . . I would trust or look to for advice." What the lighting artist taught Janice about colors and the impact of costume design remain significant cornerstones of her performing company's success today. The fact that Gerard is "resourceful" represents a cornerstone of the good relations that he shared with all three of these female artistes and their professional journey. Hanna, the former dance department director, explained: "I feel if I said Gerard . . . I'm doing this dance and I have five hundred dollars for the costumes, would you do it? I know he would find a way to do it. He's very . . . willing to find ways to accommodate choreographers."

According to Hanna, this ability comes from the fact that Gerard is "a creative spirit himself" and wants to meet a challenge through his art.

Nikki explained that "If I were going to travel, somewhere like . . . Thailand . . . and if I went up to him and I was like Gerard, you know, I was thinking about doing Thailand and blah, blah, blah, blah, I have a feeling he would start talking to me about the place and things that I should see." This was the impression that Gerard made on the dancer and choreographer as someone who was well traveled and informed from his visits to different countries. It is also the reason why Nikki, from Southern University, felt comfortable inviting Gerard to her home and walking him through the rooms so that he could give her good design ideas for the space.

But behind all of this sophistication of taste and perspective, the women intimated, it is Gerard's ability to feel comfortable in any setting that is most appreciated by his associates. When he stayed at Nikki's home for one night, he made sure that she got all the ingredients for the dishes that he would prepare for their dinner. She recollected that "he . . . gave me a grocery list . . . and we went shopping and then he came back and fixed meals for us." Nikki reported that the meal "was wonderful" and that she enjoyed sharing the home cooked food together. Nikki also remembered that Gerard just "made himself at home" and his flexible attitude just seemed to say: "whatever you have I'll be comfortable [with]. I know this is your mom's room and she is not here now and the curtains don't match, but it's okay."

The Method Behind the Madness

A philosophy that is continually fueled by the belief that one must be intent on improving your skills and awareness of the world around you centers this lighting artist and teacher of young designers. From very early on in his career, when he was in high school, Gerard knew that he wanted to be in the entertainment industry and that he should be a cornerstone in the field where he chose to make his mark. Setting off on the professional journey with the support of a famous playwright who had won international acclaim, Gerard has found himself writing the lighting design curriculum for a university in his native land where he is "all but laying down the concrete" to establish the first ever training program for undergraduate students in the island's history.

What has led him along the many roads that he has traveled to this point in his career? He talked about the "spirituality" of the work that he does, describing the process as having "angels" who guided his choices beyond doing the technical steps that must be completed in order for a lighting design to work on stage. Yes, Gerard admitted, there is the initial "fear" about starting a new design, choosing the cues on which the lights are programmed to go on and off, and putting up the show in the limited time that budget constraints always demand from a designer. But, he insisted, there is always a moment when "something" takes over and guides the way in which a lighting plot is executed from the "first mark" on the blank paper, or the first "stroke" that the computer software program makes. This moment of "inspiration" is not premeditated or anticipated by the artist, it is a gift from an unknown source that is welcomed and appreciated every single time that it is offered to the hard working lighting artist. Gerard waits patiently for the stroke of insight about a play or a character or a theme in the production, to inform his choice for positioning lights and the colors that he chooses to "paint" the canvas of the stage and actors.

How does this approach to working with lights, the way that an artist works with paints, affect the way that Gerard trains his students? He believes that he works to bring out "the artist" in each person that he instructs. The lighting artist is not interested in people who like to manipulate machines and turn out traditional lighting plots. The master designer is convinced that school is a place to experiment with attitudes to the lighting designer's work, to make mistakes in the process of mounting a production, and to learn time management skills. On and off stage the international artist is adamant that students who graduate from his program in lighting design leave with a strong ability to work artistically within a time frame and a budget. "Time is money, money is time," he constantly harps to his students. He has graduated people who now are working in the theater production industry, working with rock and roll touring groups, teaching, or working in companies that need several shows designed and lighted each season. In all four cases Gerard boasted that his students are ready for the challenge and take it on with confidence and dexterity as artists, technicians, and managers with experience.

If Gerard could arrange his career to suit his tastes he would take on professional gigs as a lighting designer and then hire apprentices and engage graduate students to work with him to get shows produced. He admitted that he cannot have "the best of two worlds" while he is in an academic environment. Short of going out on his own as a producer and designer, he takes his students on professional assignments so that they can get "real world" experience before leaving their university training program. The students get firsthand experience that helps them to understand how to compress several hours of work into one hour, if the situation demands, in order to meet the rehearsal and opening night schedule that is organized by the producers.

One of his students traveled with Gerard to his native country in order to set up lights for a show a few years ago. They were delayed on another island en route to their destination, and lost two days of production time by the time they finally arrived in the country. Gerard and his graduate student, Rodney, were enlisted to hang lights and run the dress rehearsal with the actors and musicians in a main stage production within the short window of time that was left on the production schedule. Gerard said Rodney did very well under the pressure to hang lights, run the rehearsal, and reposition some instruments to get the best effects possible with the many hues of skin shades that the cast of singers presented.

This was a trial by fire in Gerard's estimation and Rodney, who got the chance to train under those strenuous conditions, came through with flying colors. Gerard took Rodney's success at hanging lights and calling the cues for the show as a feather in his cap as a teacher. It proved to him that his philosophy for training students in practical situations was further support for insisting that they understand how much success in the entertainment business demands training and talent. He always tells his apprentices that they need stamina in order to do well if they choose to earn their living in this career. "Every day is a long day" in Gerard's experience, and so in his estimation the young in age, and at heart, are the best suited to the profession.

Travel is a big part of the work that Gerard has to manage in order to get his designs into the theaters and sites where he is hired to show his work. While he joked that he has "bought luggage" since his schedule for the last two years has included stops in Vancouver, Spain, and Brazil, he also admitted that "this is the life" that one chooses when you decide to take on the world of international entertainment. This accepting attitude is informed by his earliest memories of going to school on the English language speaking island in the Caribbean where he started his academic training. Back then, he recalled, he studied "world geography" and then went on to work for an airline that gave him the opportunity to travel the world and interact with people from many different backgrounds. Making the world his own place was part of the training from his twenties.

Gerard believes that this "broad perspective" on nations and cultures gives him and other artists from his native land an "edge" when dealing with different countries and their cultural styles. This multicultural perspective also distinguishes his work when it is viewed in contrast to designs presented by other lighting specialists from the USA and other countries. Nikki, his colleague from Southern University, remembered the impact of the work that Gerard produced when he did the lighting design for a Brazilian group that was visiting their campus during the master designer's tenure as an assistant professor. Without seeing the group perform, Gerard came up with a composition that suited and enhanced the skin tones of the company members when they presented. He brought out the strengths of the production through his awareness of mask work that was honed on the island where he grew up and studied costume production with a famous designer whose work won him a contract with the Olympics committee.

Another source of inspiration for the designer's work comes from the stability that the "family connection" of artists, producers, and actors provided him over time. There is always someone who Gerard meets at a conference presentation, say the one he appeared at in Spain in 2010, who eventually connects him with another person in another country or production. The colleagues who Gerard met in Spain wanted him to work on a production of Aida in the coming years. He is longing to return to Cartagena where the conference was staged because he visited many beautiful theaters and performance spaces. He isn't deterred by the fact that the theaters all seem to use European equipment on their stages. He explained that learning the equipment and studying the best use of the lights will be another opportunity to improve his skills and enhance his ability to communicate with yet another culture in the world.

In the long view, Gerard has hopes that he can eventually leave the entertainment business and settle on a "tea farm" somewhere like the "Himalayas." He sees this as a just reward for anyone who wants to walk away, "not linger" in the entertainment industry, after they have done many years of hard and rewarding service. Yes, indeed, he is proud to have trained many successful designers and traveled across the world to hang lights in beautiful theaters and performance spaces, but there comes a time when one must step out of the ring and recuperate from the blistering pace of meeting deadlines.

With this finale to his career in mind, Gerard described the time that he is spending in his native land as a dress rehearsal for the third act in his career. He is passing on his experience in professional production and making sure that he and others who have been on the "main stage" of the theater environment put the next chapter of the country's artistic development in the capable hands of well-trained young people. Gerard wants the best for these graduates in the same way that he had high expectations for the students who he met and trained at schools in the USA. He expects these Caribbean students to learn to enjoy traveling the world and to bring their brand of lighting aesthetic to others who they meet and study with in different sites. In the same way that Gerard met a mentor when he was in high school and gained the writer's financial and emotional support so that he could leave his country and study in the USA, Gerard hopes that his students on the island will find their champions for growth and evolution early in their careers. He also wishes that the young artists will be taken in by creative professionals who people their world in and beyond the island.

Cutting the Path

A description of Gerard's attitude to teaching at this point in his career would have to include his comment that he "still like[s] the teaching thing" because "it keeps you sharp, keeps you aware of new innovations." He began his teaching career while he was a director of the state of the art theater in his hometown soon after studying for his first degree in the USA. Making the choice to connect with the University Arts Collective on the island, he began offering internships to the students who were working on a degree at the island's then only university. This experience in teaching served Gerard well when he "got the ambition to start a master's program" and returned to school to earn his master's degree at Theater University in the USA. He explained that "when I went to grad[uate] school and I was asked to teach the entry level classes in design, that further gave me the opportunity to explore the options [of teaching] and that went relatively well, so one thing led to the other" and he kept on with the university teaching career.

Looking back on the long road that led to his present position as the creator of the first lighting design program at a new university on the island of his birth, Gerard explains the central guiding philosophy that organizes all his work on a production. "Organization and planning. It never stops, no matter what the scale of the production is, you still have to plan it out." And there are other important elements that have to be considered, he added: "You have to . . . know what the budget is, work on that budget, even if the budget is zero in some cases. If you're pulling stuff from stock [properties and lighting equipment]. You have to know how to work within the parameters of the project and plan it well."

Considering that "it's a matter of scale" and that "once you understand the scale with which you're working on or with, everything will fall in line," the designer emphasized. With this mantra in the heads of all his crew members, Gerard leads his students and production team to work on all the details that will impact the final presentation that audiences see at a performance.

Once graduate school was over Gerard decided to go to New York and try his hand as a professional lighting designer. It was his luck that the work he had done with the internationally renowned playwright from his home island had already opened the doors to a network of theaters and practitioners who hired him and recommended him to other organizations in his field. This was a short run, though, since Theater University called Gerard back to fill a teaching post as a lecturer for three years before he moved on to Southern University. As he reflected on his work at both institutions of higher education, one in the north and the other in the south of the USA, Gerard explained that he now understood that "whether you are a lecturer [or an assistant professor], it's the same amount of teaching that you have to do." He gives his students the same amount of time and attention under both contracts.

The Island Lighting Agenda

In his present position as the creator of the syllabus for the new lighting design curriculum at the university on his native island, Gerard is confronted with the challenge of "doing a great deal of paperwork because once we began [the journey of getting the curriculum approved], the accreditation counselor kind of switched its gears and wanted a different set of paperwork and . . . the performing arts program got right in

line with that." The change of government on the island, and admin-
istrators at the university, proved a challenge to the process that the
newly formed performing arts department leaders had to complete. The
lighting designer, at this point of his involvement with the university,
sees his work as bringing together the elements to "start up a lighting
program when none existed before." Gerard believes that on the island
"most people seem to understand what dance needs, what music will
need," but must be led down a very carefully laid path of education in
order for them to understand the needs of the technician who illumi-
nates the stage for dancers and musicians and other performers.

What has been most gratifying to Gerard about this journey in
creating the lighting design program for his country is the fact that
he is "bringing my own experiences and particularly with a kind of
a Caribbean feel to it because that's important to the program here,
that it has a Caribbean flavor for want of a better word." By this flavor
Gerard elucidated that "Caribbean body movement is going to respond
to light in a much different way [than European, light skinned tones]."
Based on Gerard's professional experience, "skin tones are completely
different [than the tones that are mostly represented in North American
performance programs]." Gerard continued to describe his approach:
"I mean, most North American companies, from dancing [programs],
might get a few people of [darker] color, but [on the island] everybody
is of color." By this he is referring to the many hues that skin shades
from dark chocolate to café au lait represent. The lighting director has
decided to "deal" with this reality of the diversity of skin tones by offering a module that trains designers to "light for Caribbean skin tones" in
lighting for dance companies, for example. The students would also be
exposed to the ways in which they would collaborate with the "costume
designer and the choreographer" to ensure that the color composition
that the stage presents is one that is harmonious.

The Bare Facts of Lighting Magic

Gerard is also concerned that he teach the students in this new lighting
program about the "behavior of that particular kind of light or color"
which enhances a Caribbean performance so that they "could understand

how to use it even better and combine it with a bunch of other stuff" on a lighting panel. His attitude to teaching lighting is that the teacher should "strip it down to the physics and then bring [the students] back up to speed quickly 'cause they understand color but they [are] not quite sure why they use what they use" in a lighting design plot.

This is important to Gerard because he remembers that when he was working on productions on the island before going off to the USA for training in a theater program, that his local colleagues "were using things that you would out of necessity but you weren't quite sure why, but then once you kind of understood the tenets" of applying that particular instrument to a design, you could develop on that knowledge. He also explained that "a whole bunch of LED equipment, you know, energy saving equipment out there now . . . it's getting better and better and better in how to apply that for what we need to do" in a Caribbean context.

A Mentor to the Mentees

Colleagues who worked with Gerard at Southern University and the director who still hires him on the island after twenty years' worth of productions speak with a unanimous voice about his "nurturing quality" and the strong trait of "helping students." Hanna, at Southern University, believes that Gerard would best fit a unit where he is on a production team and has apprentices working with him. All the colleagues who have worked with Gerard in his capacity as a lighting director say that he is concerned about students seeing "practical applications" and hairing "hands on" experience in the field of lighting design and stage management. Nikki, the other colleague at Southern University, is also aware that students will always refer to Gerard as a "mentor and teacher." She is also clear that Gerard was interested in students being able to "create some depth" when they mounted a lighting design. He would encourage students to read widely, and to have an appreciation for the world around them so that they could bring that sensibility to their work on the stage.

Since Gerard sees himself as someone who is "practicing World theatre," he always exposes his students to the places and people who are part of his professional world. When he described his tenure at Institute of Theater University he said that the students had "to work with me on something. So they get the process in the first two years, that they understand the process [of mounting their lighting designs]. Then they actually start to work with it and with me in years three and four" of their program. This ensured that the students were "as prepared as you can get with them" so that they could take up the professional opportunities that presented themselves soon after they graduated from the university program.

There was a company near the campus that was willing to let the school program "borrow its equipment and they were quite happy . . . because they know . . . [the students] would come and [and join the company as professionals and] they don't have to train them." Since lighting equipment evolves every six or eight weeks it was a good idea for the students, "a nice kind of interlacing" with the professional community, and a situation which Gerard describes as "very unusual for any school."

When Gerard moved on from the Institute of Theater to take up the consulting post at the new university on his native island he made sure that "even from some distance . . . that those [students] who were left in the lighting program got into . . . various jobs." This was possible because of the strong relationship that Gerard had built with a lighting and production company in the state where Institute of Theater was located. He reported that "they've always been very good about hiring the students. . . . so almost to a man they're all at work at [the production company] and out on the road."

It is important to this instructor that he involve his students in his professional productions. Gerard emphasized that "every time I've taken a grad[uate] student . . . I think in one case I had an undergrad[uate] to come into the West Indian Dance Theater's 50th anniversary," it has enhanced the student's learning experience. This is one other way, according to the award winning designer, to develop a personal relationship with the students besides meeting them during office hours when they "have problems and are always dropping by . . . asking about things pertaining to the projects they're working on or the designs that they're working on."

After many years of meeting deadlines for productions under less than perfect conditions, Gerard holds his students to a high aesthetic bar regardless of the circumstances in which they find themselves working. He once explained to a student that "a lot of us create under that very special moment when a lot of the river, the confluences come together, and something inspires you to do something you hadn't planned." This is the point at which the designer is encouraged to recognize that the new plan may "actually work even better" than the one that was the initial idea for the show. Gerard insists that this inspired moment in production is "that sort of thing you can't deny."

Challenges to the Ideal

There are as many gifts as there are challenges when Gerard works with students. He mentioned one student who left the training program at Institute of Theater before he completed his assignments for the degree. Gerard sighed when he explained that the student "knows what he needs to do to finish [the requirements] . . . but if he does it [is] another matter." The student, however, did manage to "achieve far more than what he set out to do" as far as employment, for somebody who just left a lighting program.

Another instance of the kind of speed bumps that students encountered while Gerard was teaching was the reality of "politics" in an institution. Gerard related: "They quickly kind of understand that they need to sort of play a game to survive and to get the job and . . . that it is more cut throat competition than they had imagined." The lighting designer confided that "no amount of talk will prepare [the students for the professional world], but they have been able to handle it very, very well." As Gerard recalled, only one student "actually called me back when he was having some sort of issues with an employer about what he was hired to do." After some "chit chat" about the office politics at the job site, Gerard encouraged the young man to "go in and say something" to his employer and "he went in and spoke and things were all sorted out in twenty-four hours." In Gerard's estimation, this was another example of how the faculty and Institute of Theater "try to help" students, and it is a good recommendation for the "studio type class where it is just two or three people," in the lighting major. Such a small group of students to attend to during the program allows a more "one on one" relationship that can be beneficial to the student long after they have graduated.

Finally, Gerard described the situation where he had to "cut" a student from the lighting program. The facts showed that the student "was taking a very long time to get [the ideas for the lighting designs]" completed. Gerard did not think that it was "a good idea [for him] to continue in the program" and none of the reasons had to do with the student's ability. In fact, Gerard explained it wasn't about whether the student had "talent" but rather, the challenge of working in technical careers where "you have three times as short [as you want] to be able to pull [the show] off." Gerard just thought that the student needed "to go away and rethink it to see if this is what he really wants to do . . . because he will be returning to it after a considerable amount of time." In consideration of the "health of the program" the teachers had "to keep going and to keep the other students working at a pace and not waiting for somebody to catch up."

Time and Tide

If students talked about Gerard and his attitude during production, which begins 14 weeks before a show opens, they would probably refer to his concern that he stay on task and learn new things to make it easy to stay within the timeline. "The technology changes every 6–8 weeks. So there's always new stuff to play with and to get acquainted with and to apply" to a production, Gerard explained.

According to Gerard the process of being in a school environment is about "constant learning and teaching" and he believes that "the minute that you kind of say, well, there's not much more to learn, that's dangerous 'cause there's always new stuff coming down the pipeline and with great frequency these days." The designer has taken the attitude that it's best "to keep up" with the changes even though "it's a challenge."

Gerard insisted that "every day is a long day" in this production business. In his experience of thirty plus years, "you come . . . for your 8:00 class and you're [in the theater] until five, and then you have production meetings from five to six, and then you try to inhale some dinner and start rehearsal from seven to eleven."

This kind of grind does not let up as long as you are in the production program. Gerard also added that "if you're mounting a production then you're working on the weekends as well." It very seldom varies when you get a job in a road show or a professional theater. This is the work ethic that he builds his students to sustain while he is training them.

One good thing about being young and involved in this production discipline is that "they have the stamina to do it because it really takes a great deal of time and not just for the backstage folks but . . . on stage as well." Gerard philosophized about the need for balance in the technician's life if he or she is going to make it a lasting career. He cites one experience with a student who graduated: "One grad student came in [at twenty-three, if not twenty-four] and still is managing [to keep in the profession], you know, doing what he has to do and he's still in the rock and roll industry." This is impressive to Gerard because that industry is a "really rough one and a lot of traveling and being away from family, but he's managed to hold it together very well. [He and his wife are] still together."

Besides the fact that young people need to "strike that balance" between personal and professional life, Gerard also believes that it's important for them to know that they "can make a comfortable living. That's the important thing for most young people going into this industry now is whether they make a living out of this." This theme of longevity is reflected later on in Gerard's comments to students in his native land as they were about to enter the training program at the new university. Gerard reported that:

> I made it . . . very clear to them [that] this is a long haul. This is an investment in yourself. . . . which they hadn't thought of it [in] that way. So the thing is to make sure that they're well prepared, I would say, and that they have been able to manage their time, get them to understand how to manage their day and still be able to get the rest required to face the next long day.

This approach to training professionals goes with the knowledge that Gerard acquired after working with the present group of elders in the theater production community for three decades. He reported that "now there's a carnival almost every month" taking place "up and down the Caribbean or in the [places where there are] lots of West Indians." This is the way in which Gerard and his colleagues have been able to assess the level of need for professionals who can work on the stage productions throughout the year. It is clear to this cadre of theater practitioners that "sound and light [are] a close component in the carnival and in most of the festivals" that are celebrated in the West Indian Diaspora. So, as a result, Gerard is placing his bets on the high demand that will be put on the graduates of the new university's production program. In his estimation, "once we have a standardization in what the training is and what the outcomes should be," with regard to a lighting designer, then "the bar is going to be set and raised" so that professional technicians can be employed to do all the work that is already available for them as lighting designers.

The Method Is the Meaning

Gerard explains his approach to lighting for productions as a "need to express and support what is happening on stage." Since lighting is "not something that is like a text that is there, lighting and sound, they happen when they happen and then that's the end of that until the next time," Gerard pushes his students to think with the aid of images. Even though Gerard sees this task as a difficult one, his passion is expressed in his belief that "it's something that I don't think I would rather not do. I don't think I could do something else with my life."

When his students begin to plan lighting designs for productions of plays, Gerard points their attention to the details of the plot. He explained that "each individual moment [in a live performance] is different every single time, and that is very exciting." He trains his students to understand that "every way a line gets delivered [in a play], and the way that that line is lit as it is delivered is different."

This is why the master designer insists that his students learn to handle a camera and be "able to take your own photographs and . . . know when to take the shot as well because you know what the moment is where the lights are going to change." This is part of the process of learning to be a professional. Gerard drills his students in understanding that "it makes common sense to be able to document your work . . . so when you got to put a portfolio together or update your portfolio you have your own stuff for it." This underscores the belief that the lighting experience is ephemeral, like an actor's performance, and the only way to have someone outside the show see the effects that were created on stage is to capture the moment of the lighting effect on camera.

Gerard is known to "encourage the students to take photography class" so that they "understand how a camera works and how to use it." He reminds students that "relying on other people would involve some kind of cost" and that "investing in your own camera and taking your [pictures] . . . just makes perfect sense." This follows logically from the belief that the production process for the lighting designer is so much "like television, a story board, a series of images or photographs." Gerard is happy if students present "hand sketches, [or] some of them are using electronic visualization through different computer programs," so that they "develop some visual image to show the directors and give the costume designers their sketches" for the design effects that they want to create on stage.

One of Gerard's colleagues at Southern University remembered clearly that when she was working on the production about Frida Kahlo, she "had all these ideas in my brain but I couldn't get them to conceptualize for this stage." She found that talking with Gerard "artistically and [about] what symbolically would work helped me to flush out those ideas for the dance." The final production evolved into a presentation where it "Started with pure white costumes, very plain, and as [Kahlo's] work and her life got more complicated with the issues she was dealing with, more costume pieces and color were added to the pallet and [Gerard] was able to contribute to that narrative through his lighting."

Decisions on the aesthetic of the look of the show have to be made when the actors and costumes and dramatic line through all come together. As Gerard explained:

> "You have a limited window in which to get all these looks that you've been planning put into the computer or whatever console it is that you might be using. . . . because it is a tight time crunch, you have to be prepared. . . . because you cannot do that on the fly, in the short window that you have."
>
> The moment of making a smooth flow of color and all the other elements of the production come together is a result of working with the costume designer and finding out if "the colors you picked are working properly with

these costumes and make up and see if it is being used well in each moment, how is each cue proportional to support what is happening on stage whether it is choreography or a text, that has to be considered carefully."

Gerard insists that all his productions, whether student directed or a professional piece, "must look good, it must look beautiful."

Hindsight Is Perfect

Looking back at his journey with students, Gerard described his students at Institute of Theater as "bright kids, very intelligent people that can have conversations about all kinds of things and not just theater." This is a very important aspect of his evaluation of the quality of his students since Gerard believes that "everything impacts your thought and your thoughts are what you bring to the drafting table when it's time to produce a design." Based on his own experiences as a world traveler, Gerard appreciated the fact that the students "all travel" because he believed that "most Americans are a little bit afraid to travel" and his students, in contrast, "get out there and go to the four corners of the earth when they can."

Gerard also reflected on all the students who are already employed and are enjoying a career in their chosen field of lighting design. He beamed with enthusiasm when he explained that at "this stage, [it] is the legacy that you pass on to students, to other people, other young artists that you're trying to change" for the good that really matters to him. He feels "very, very proud" that students who have worked with him are "now doing this, this, and this" and stacking up their credits as professionals. He knows that it makes a great difference to the graduates that they "can do this professionally" and after all their investment in being trained that they "don't have to work in a bank" in order to maintain themselves. The fact that he could name the sites where his students were employed including the "Mary Kay Industrial, J-Lo Tour, Rock 'n Roll type things, R. Kelly" and other popular entertainment productions, is testimony to the close relationships that Gerard maintains with his graduates and the prestige assignments that they are able to maintain in their careers.

Richard

Deep
Dark
Smoldering   With passion
Unlike
The sounds
That roll   Rumble   Ricochet off
Of
Instruments
For   Human   Hands that
Caress   And Bless

Quiet
Though not   Still
Hearing   Though still
Listening   For lyrics   In
Words   In   Movements
In between   Breaths   And   Still learning
To be   Calm

Catching   Breath as
It rolls out   In words   And sighs   And untold
Dreams

Chapter Five

Richard's Song

The first instrument that Richard remembered playing was a piano. According to Winston, one of his close friends and musician colleagues, he had "very strict parents" who insisted that he practice regularly. Ray, another good friend from his hometown, remembered him "as a piano player" who was known for "playing 'legit' classical music." By the time Richard graduated from high school in the Caribbean island where he grew up, he was playing the acoustic bass and then began working his way into positions as an arranger for steelbands and a composer of music. Ray also recalled that Richard "started playing the bass, because he knew the music 'from the bottom up' loved it, he started to read and he did a lot of recordings with a lot of calypsonians" who included famous people on the local music scene on the island. Eventually Richard would perform as a pannist, steel pan instrumentalist, and bassist at the Lincoln Center in New York with other famous musicians who had earned the right to be called exemplars of Caribbean music. But the journey to the occasion at the famous performance venue in New York City was a long one that began with his professional development in calypso tents on his native island where he honed his skills as a competent sideman for calypsonians during the carnival season and for popular singers during the rest of the year. Richard built a sturdy reputation for his musical skills and his leadership abilities.

Richard remembered that early in his career he was working as a librarian at the national office for one of the daily newspapers in his home country and doing music and theatre on the side for several outfits. He performed as an actor and wrote music for a television workshop company, the first in the country, and other music organizations where he had opportunities to play his bass or piano and sing with the members. After a few years of doing this kind of double duty, working in the office and playing for different bands and choirs in the evening, he quit his day job and performed music full-time for several years before deciding to go to a school in the USA to continue his studies.

A professional musician who returned to Richard's home in the Caribbean after earning his living in North America for several years met with Richard at his home and told him about the International Jazz School, a fictitious name, in Massachusetts. The school had a reputation "as a conservatory" where "prominent jazz musicians have graduated. They had curriculum that was set up to help musicians be proficient instrumentalists and good arrangers in jazz, blues, and R&B (rhythm and blues)." Biars, Richard's mentor, listened to Richard talk about his goals as a musician and his longing to take the calypso form of music and do more interesting things with the themes and arrangements that the calypsonians had created in their original compositions. The professional musicians agreed that a choice to North America for the purpose of continuing his studies was a good choice for Richard.

Richard also recalled that Leezan, a returning architect who also played music professionally on the island, was one of the major influences of his vision for the kind of Caribbean music that he wanted to create and play. Richard reminisced:

> I think this was in the early 70s, [Leezan] was one of those . . . [at the forefront] of jazz movement, calypso jazz movement and [he had a] very clear concept of using calypso . . . to influence his compositions and [a very clear concept of using calypso and folk rhythms in his compositions and arrangements] . . . his

concept was very Caribbean . . . very Trinidadian. . . . So [Leezan] was very good at communicating that . . . kind of intellectual [music]. . . . So by going to hear him play and getting to know him and then playing with him, I [gained] this respect for taking and using [Caribbean] music as a resource, a wellspring to do all this other stuff with and [Leezan] is great at doing that and a lot of musicians around him at that time [shared and experimented with a similar concept].

The Proof of the Pudding

Two words characterize the personality and communication style of Richard, according to his closest companions Ray and Winston. Ray talked about Richard's nature as being "quiet" and "calm." This longtime friend and band member also mentioned the fact that "sometimes [Richard] is very laid-back" and "most people will . . . say that he is very nice." Ray also mentioned that other musicians find Richard easy to work with and are concerned that his music "presentation" is always at the highest standard possible. A native of Richard's home island as well, Ray explained that Richard "always tries to present what he is doing the best way possible . . . he is very much concerned" that listeners get the best impression of Caribbean music when they attend his performances, school demonstrations, or workshops. Since Richard is the only other musician that Ray will work with since arriving in the USA, he has long distanced himself from other island natives because of the difference in their work ethic and criteria for performance quality. He knows that it is a sign of the deep respect that he has for Richard. Ray explained:

> The reason that I play with him is because I enjoy playing with him, I enjoy his company whenever we are together, we always talk about music . . . [he always tells me to] check this CD out, or I heard this piece of music on the radio, check it out and there's this program next week. . . . Bet your life, that if he tells me that, it is something good to listen to.

Richard maintains a work ethic that states to other musicians, "be on time, dress well, present yourself well, and the product will [sell] itself." Ray observed that the depth of the relationship that he has shared with

Richard is based on this sincere respect for music as a lifestyle and the fact that he believed that Richard is "good people" who knows how to lead people and get the job done at a high standard.

It was a surprise when Ray found out that when he "went to [Richard's] home . . . he had a picture of me on the wall as you come in the front door," and this was the first time that it was clear to Ray that Richard "considers me as a friend." This sincere friend has weathered many musical storms with Richard as they tried to build a musical tradition in their new hometown in the USA, and he has only one criticism of Richard after many interactions with him. Ray admits that "sometimes I think that he is too easy, he could be a little more demanding" of his musicians and the people who employ his band on gigs. Coming from the perspective of Richard, who recounted that "most of my friends are longtime friends," it would be hard to ignore such an assessment from Ray. Richard would count Ray among the people that he considers "close" to him and admitted that "if we talk, it is because there is something we are working on, there's a gig or performance or something" that demanded more than an email communication.

Winston, a longtime friend and music associate in Richard's life, also uses the word "respect" when he reflects on the experiences that he has shared with Richard since they met at the International Jazz School. He considers Richard a "close, close friend" and thinks that the fact that Richard invited him to play on his first CD was one of the symbols of the high regard with which Richard held this veteran musician from his native island. The other experience that has influenced the way in which Winston has come to consider Richard's character is in the interpersonal exchange that they had regarding the invitation that was extended to him to be a part of this research project about Richard's journey as a professor at the International Jazz School. Richard was "nonchalant" in his mention of the project and the fact that Winston would be contacted by the researcher to do an interview. He never explained that the interview would focus on Richard and his journey in the USA. Just like Ray was surprised to find a picture of himself hanging in Richard's house, Winston was taken off guard in the way that he found himself ranked in his friend's personal network. Winston was "happy" to talk about

Richard and impressed that he was only one of two people that Richard recommended to reflect on his career to date. It gave Winston new perspective on the regard with which Richard held him and his insights about his life and struggles since his student days at the International Jazz School.

According to Ray, among the challenges that Richard faces as he tries to work well with his musicians, students, and colleagues, and produce original music, is the reality that includes the composer "being single" and having to take care of his home, his mortgage, and his professional responsibilities in and out of school, without any support at home or from his family who live outside the city and country. According to Richard, who would rather "stay home and write" every day but is driven by the "responsibility [of teaching]" and believing that "I have to show up," this is how he functions. He has established the tradition that "I am one of those people who shows up . . . for class and you know the students know I will be there instead of them waiting [and I don't turn up]" to work with them. So this puts an additional burden on him as a wage earner and writer.

When it comes to representing the music that Richard cares about, Ray told a story that depicted the kind of resistance that the band leader has to face when he goes out to share his music at social events. Ray described the incident that led him to understand that: "I know for a fact that Richard wanted to present this [original] music. The hardest thing when you want to do that is to get musicians that are responsible, that can play well, that will show up on time, that will prepare themselves for what has to be done."

When they were hired to play at an event Ray remembered how sad it made him that he was "there with him . . . and [Richard] has his music and we are playing, and we end up playing some sad North American music on the gig" to please the employers who are not interested in Richard's original music from his native country.

Admittedly, Richard is a "stickler" for well-rehearsed performances and music that is authentic to the Caribbean tradition that he believes that he represents. Even when he had to play with bands on road gigs, he was concerned about the toll that staying in hotels and traveling on buses would have on his health and general well-being.

He still wanted to "respect [the musician's] music" that he was being asked to play in the face of the other obstacles that traveling and performing represented. He insisted that he was not only "eating well and enjoying music" but "growing, learning from this person" who he was working with and learning the "tradition" that inspired the leader's creativity.

Learning continues to be a hallmark of the way in which Richard approaches his teaching and composing assignments. He stated that he was "still trying to be true to my own traditions, yet embrace as many of the 'Diasporic' traditions that I could grab and add to the mix." He continued with this insight: "I understand what African musicians are doing with their own music and the marriage with Afro-American popular music, the same with Latin American musicians and yet they still have such a strong identity."

Richard explained:

> . . . I say to my students that yes, true I come from this particular tradition but I am trying to learn and understand about all of these other traditions that I see are becoming very much a part of this global music mix. I think you can just be so much of a better musician, better person, if you respect and pay attention and you learn the culture and the people and understand them well.

He talked about one musician who inspired him in to broaden his musical horizons when he described the man's approach to making compositions and arrangements. Richard said: "What I like most about him is that he is willing to always jump off the bridge and not worry about where he falls . . . he is very rooted in his music, knows it inside and out." The nature of such a risk-taker is a contrast to Richard's approach which is somewhat more academic in his eyes. He explained: "I'm not like that [musician] yet, maybe because I am always studying in this academic environment because I always figure there is so much more to learn." Richard believes that such an approach to music making is a "gift" and the musician he describes is inspiring because he "is willing to run with [his impulses] . . . to just jump in. Just do it . . . [since] he doesn't want to have to think about it too much." And the result of the response to the creative forces in the musician is that "whenever you hear it, [the music] is happening, it is refreshing." Richard, the lifelong learner, is ever watchful for these manifestations of talent and creativity within the musical genre he aspires to represent and advance.

Home Away From Home

The early years in the cold North American climate were not easy for Richard. He regretted that "it wasn't the best experience at the start" since he not only had to contend with the fact that he was an older student and set in many ways than most of his classmates at the jazz school, but he also had to adjust to the fact that he had given up a thriving music career in his native land in order to broaden his music education. He didn't let his music career lag while he attended classes at the school as a way of countering the kind of discouragement that could have overtaken his attitude. And so the burden of looking for professional work and playing at the level he was accustomed to in his homeland became an additional stressor during his years as an international student at the school.

Richard recounted ruefully that "[the city where I was staying] at the time did not have quite the active music scene as I thought it would be. The school provides this statement about the students doing concerts every week at school", Richard reflected cynically, and so "you get . . . misinformed about this experience about what was happening in the clubs, what kind of money you take home from this [kind of gig]." As a professional working musician you quickly learn that "you have to spend money on advertising" and that kind of expenditure "became a reality once I got out of school." Then, once he graduated the next set of demands quickly made themselves known as "you are no longer paying for school but now you have to think of people" who have to be paid when they do a gig with your band.

Fortunately for Richard, when he got to the music school "there were really no great pan players and I wanted to be able to play with people who did play the pan." So he began studying the pan on his own and playing on gigs as his reputation as a competent multi-instrumentalist got around. Ray, his friend from the days on their native island, smiled as he recalled that "it was a good opportunity because there wasn't much steel drum players around here in [the city] at the time. . . . From there . . . [Richard] started arranging for some [steel]band." It was also during this period that Richard learned "so much about contracts, and technical riders and making travel expenses"; he also learned a hard lesson: "The first year I had to pay taxes from money that was paid to me." Richard had to learn the music business fast and he had to get accustomed to keeping records on social security numbers for transient band members and other people who were part of the regular core group of musicians. While the stress was difficult to manage at first, Richard insisted that he made sure that the music was "happening in that environment," and that his reputation for delivering a high quality sound was not ever disputed among musicians or the employers who booked the band. He reported that in those early years as a band leader he had to find a way to do the business end and "still maintain my composure and still seem like a decent human being" to his band members and his employers.

The first band that Richard organized was composed of musicians who all came "from [Caribbean] islands and they were playing calypso and we had been playing for a while and . . . we were real tight, we were good friends apart from the music." This experience was happening at the same time that Richard was being exposed to "great musicians" at the International Jazz School. There were

> . . . some good teachers, and some [not so good ones] too. But great musicians, talented musicians from all over the world [were performing and teaching at the school], and I envisioned myself continuing in that environment to be able to perform and write at the level of musicianship [that he experienced as a student and performer at the school.]

After graduating from the famous music school, Ray remembered that Richard "was also working part-time in . . . the registrar's office" and that he formed a jazz band. This "sextet comprised of steel drums and regular drum sets, electric bass, and piano, keyboard" and on some occasions they included "percussion and a vocalist." It was at this time that Richard "started doing . . . arrangements and he would play them

[at] gigs." The sextet also "did a couple concerts," "programs," and "things at schools." Ray, a longtime collaborator with Richard, is convinced that his friend Richard "loved arranging" and that "even in [the Caribbean] he had some affiliations with . . . the band [that won several national steelband competitions]." So while Richard described himself as someone who still has "a reservation to . . . call myself a pan player" he has put in a lot of time developing his skill on the instrument and earning the right to teach it at the International Jazz School. His dedication to promoting the steelpan instrument has led to the creation of two ensembles for steelpans and now the opportunity for students to study the steelpan as a principal instrument.

Close Encounters of the Musical Kind

A decision to "broaden" his musical experience led Richard back to school to study musicology. As he described his decision-making process, he explained that he had to "decide how I wanted to fit into this evolving music scene in the city where I was a student". His review of his choices as a professional musician led him "to get some more knowledge" and "to study some more [at an academic institution]." He was still "actively playing music" as he worked to "broaden" his experience in the areas of composition. The hunger for more knowledge about styles of music and composition skills was also fueled by the fact that Richard realized he "didn't have that kind of support from the informal teachers in [his native land]." Many musicians he met early in his career in his native island did not freely share information and the people he met early on in the music industry, the elders who he saw as "teachers because they were older musicians," actually "did not know more than [he] did" and that they "did not impart knowledge as freely . . . [were] scared to share [or even] say this is what I've been doing, this is the book I've been using and give me the book" so that he could study and improve his skills. Because Richard was clear about the direction he wanted to develop his composition skills as early as the 1970s, and that it was imperative for him to "stretch out of [the island] and pick the things that I like from North America" so that he could mix it with Caribbean influences and ensure that "when you hear [his music] there is no doubt about [the] . . . strong [island]" influence, he organized himself to study, play music, and earn his keep while working in a business office at a music school.

Ray, the longtime friend from back in the day on the island, understood that Richard "learned . . . the jazz and the harmony" to add to his Caribbean music, which included Latin music, "the French and the Asian influence, the Reggae from Jamaica," and the classical training that began in music lessons. School represented a laboratory experience which allowed Richard to experiment as he added new influences and got inspiration from the musicians in and out of the jazz school. Since graduating from his musicology experience, Richard feels that he's "closer now to the possibility [of creating the kind of music that he dreamed of as a new jazz student] with the experience of being in that [school] environment." The multitalented composer and musician feels that he has arrived at the place in his career where documenting "some of the ideas that I would not be able to accomplish . . . [early on] because of lack of funding and whatever the problems of getting [the ideas recorded]" and played by competent musicians is now a reality.

The Muse

Richard wants the world to know that he comes from a small English speaking island in the Caribbean. He wants his music to broadcast that "I am very proud to be [from my native country] but living in North America and see myself being able to absorb what I think is important, or the musical traditions that I think would enhance what I do." The veteran musician also wants his band members to "sound as [if] they were actually part of [his Caribbean culture]." It's important to his philosophy of making music that people listening to the players "should think . . . that's a jazz piano player playing in that environment" and not be distracted by their habits from playing North American jazz music.

When the composer talks about the source from which he gets his creative inspiration, he cites his elders in the island music that he grew up listening to and from which he learned melodies. Richard described his attitude in this way: "I think [the island musicians] have a lot of great material that never gets heard I want to be able to continue to write, that from those influences as opposed to just writing pretty, tunes that doesn't really say anything, don't really define anything about me."

It is this tradition, of listening to the old as a foundation for building the new, that influences Richard's choices when he works with his band members and students. If he is working on a composition in a rehearsal he might

> . . . play something for [the musicians] . . . on the piano and . . . play a couple of rhythms and say . . . these are some of the rhythms that I'd like you to play. And [the student pianist] may actually take a note of them, actually write them down, or go and work with them and see what those rhythms help him generate."

In Richard's ideal world it is not enough for him to play his best as a bass player and join other bands that hire him for his expertise. He has standards that he described as "continuing a tradition that you think that some others [from my native island] have been working on for many years and you'll see yourself developing this tradition." The Caribbean artist also wants "to be able to make a living and feel satisfied with [the mix of talent and compassion.]" He is particularly concerned with "[the quality of] musicians" with whom he plays. This idea of the "quality" of a musician in Richard's estimation is generated by a belief that he has "respect for all these [music] traditions, [and] other traditions that I think I need to study, I need to learn, I need to understand, I need to be able to play" in order to improve the work that he produces as a player and composer. These musical traditions include the blues and/or jazz standards of Charlie Parker, Thelonious Monk, and John Coltrane. To further elucidate his philosophy of life-long learning, Richard declared that "I know some [of the work] of these artists, I now understand . . . and respect these players and know a little bit about their repertoire. I think it makes you a really rounded and informed musician, particularly if you want to be a jazz musician and educator today."

The musicologist feels strongly that this openness to other traditions is only one of the important features of being a good musician. He espoused his need to establish the culture of "using the material, the songs, the melodies and rhythms from your own culture and background and keep . . . making sure that people hear this material" in order to advance the culture of appreciating the past in order to build a lasting future. For this reason, Richard has set a goal for his career as a composer and teacher. He elucidated on the concept that

> . . . when it comes on to figuring what you're going to be known [for], . . . the material that is going . . . to define where you've come from, or where you want to go and if you really see yourself as dedicating yourself to being a musician representing this rich Caribbean [music] then you have to know the musical sources that you are going to draw from.

So a "[major] part of our work" and here he has included other musicians who are seen as "contributing to that [tradition] too," is "doing more and more of this [fusion] music" that is grown in the Caribbean with all its influences from Africa, Spain, France, and other nations.

The work of being a symbol of this approach to diversity and inclusiveness has carried over into the service that Richard has done for the International Jazz School. He has served on a committee for inclusion and diversity that appointed the college's first "diversity officer," and has worked with others to make recommendations that will help ease the transition period that students from other nations must make if they are to be successful at the school in Massachusetts. One of the struggles has been for the recognition of the pan as a principal instrument. Richard always hoped "to be developing [his] . . . pan class beyond being just an ensemble" so that students had a wider experience of the instrument's potential for being included in the musical tool box that they could dip into when making their original scores.

A multi-year effort to get the music curriculum diversified resulted in Richard being given the task of "advertising this [pan] major and by doing a lot of personal work . . . designing the courses, finding materials, getting ideas from people who are really doing something similar" at other universities and colleges, so that he could decide what he wanted to do "in terms of shaping a program." He listed several schools that he planned to visit including "Northern Illinois and West Virginia" and "seeing what they're doing, what I don't like about it, what I like about it" and deciding whether to include or exclude his present dreams for pan majors at the International Jazz School.

The foundational belief that "once you are open to learning and experiencing a different concept" underpins the decisions that Richard makes in terms of his music career and teaching students. In the same way that he decided that working on a diversity committee at the Jazz school "was important and the experience was good" for his development, so too, he believes that students should see cross-cultural experiences as "opening [their] minds up to embracing" what is part of the North American culture. He especially encourages students to look at South American and other Latin music traditions for the experience of the new additions to the culture that is being forged around them.

The fact that Richard does not have "a whole lot of material" from his island in the Caribbean, "so much of our best music is hard to find," or that he can't say to students "go get this record, go get that record" in order to have them study the music that was produced on his native island, does not deter him from encouraging his young charges to "start getting to understand and getting to study [other music outside their first loves] and respecting it as well. Richard perseveres with this approach to teaching about the world outside the boundaries that time and experience have set up for his students because of their backgrounds. He does his cultural work in spite of the fact that "you don't reach a whole lot of people [in the international school] because they have . . . figured out they want to do this one [kind of music]. This is what is going to make . . . them successful and they want to follow this one path" in spite of the world of music that is being introduced to them in the jazz school.

The Music Is the Message

Richard is aware that he has to cue his musicians and students into his way of seeing and appreciating his ideal. He knows that words are not enough and this fact comes across when he thinks about the process of doing the interviews for this project. He reflected on the fact that "the body language" is an important part of the interaction that takes place when he tells me his story about being a musician in the USA. He was fully aware that he was "assuming that there's so many things that I don't say that you understand" because I saw the way that his body moved when he shared his ideas. I also have a fairly good idea of the music traditions that inform his repertoire of island melodies and cultural references.

Ever aware that he is communicating his background knowledge at every moment, Richard explained that there were "all the unsaid [things] . . . all the nuances, all the things that I say with my body more than . . . [what's] actually on the tape" that helped him to explain what he hopes he can communicate about his passion for his native music and the hopes that he has for exposing it to international musicians whom he encounters in his new home in the USA. Despite the fact that Richard believed that not "a lot of people are actually really interested in the information" about what he wants to create through his music, and his hopes for his students, he firmly believes that there are pockets of interest that can still be exposed to the people with a lot more information about the traditions behind the music that he promotes and the founders who are still working in that genre of music.

The seasoned musician still doesn't believe that he has "arrived [at] any synthesis that I am totally comfortable with but I think it's a work that will . . . be in progress for a long time," and he is certain that his work is about coming up "with material that I think [as a synthesis of folk and jazz and Caribbean traditions that] represents that concept very well." The ideal of the long hours of labor and experimentation with composing and arranging in Richard's mind is to "keep showcasing the work of the [island] composers whose work . . . rarely gets air play, rarely ever gets redone after they are done in the original form by these artists." What Richard is determined to do is to "take those melodies and tunes and try to refresh them, bring them in a new form" so that different artists can be exposed to them as "other types of music," and learn to "play them in different styles" so that the repertoire of music for those interested in this kind of Caribbean flavored jazz is spread abroad.

The work that best represents this effort to increase the menu of choices available to musicians in this area of style is the CD that Richard designed to "pull [old standards as] material into this concept . . . [of] a thread running through the steel, brass and iron" instruments that are generally used as filler sounds in calypsos. Rather than have the percussion "being in the background" the compositions would ensure that it "could actually have its own voice at some point of the arrangement of the composition." So Richard envisages that "there would be the instrumentation, there would be some tracks that would have brass, some tracks would be steel, some tracks would put the iron upfront as a lead instrument." Based on his love for the music that he grew up listening to and learning to play, Richard's work continues to be inspired by the belief that the original composers of his native island's music provides "material and their work . . . [is just] as good as anything" that he has "experienced" and learned to appreciate outside the home island context.

This idea of revising the standard repertoire from the calypso writers is based on Richard's guiding philosophy that "you make sure that you're centered . . . in what has shaped you culturally." From that platform of insight, the musicians who work with Richard are encouraged to see themselves "looking out and seeing how you can embrace all these other traditions and find [other] art and use that to decorate and to shape your own stuff." Richard also encourages his students "to start to think more about using rhythm as a way of expressing yourself rather than all this harmonic information that you learn in your class and [all the music from] all these great players who play all of these notes" so that they can focus on being "simple" in their approach to playing music. The veteran musician promotes the attitude among his mentees that making good music has a lot to do with "approaching life a little bit simpler" than they usually do when he encounters them in classrooms and rehearsal studios. Richard said that he is "trying to be . . . a representative of that [lifestyle]" that he believes enhances the music making that is valuable to him and his vision of excellence. Therefore, he is constantly working "to be a good . . . role model for [students]" and insists on working to be clear about "whatever I talk about musically" and that it "is kind of reflected in the way I live and the way I carry myself."

There are stories about how the students reach out to Richard when they try to learn how to create the fusion of Caribbean music styles that is the hallmark of his work. The young musicians, according to Richard, don't want to know "just the history" of the composers who they study, but how their teacher writes, arranges, and composes. The reputation that Richard has established inside and outside of the classrooms at the International Jazz School is endorsed by the kind of music accolades he has accrued over his time in the USA. One of his outstanding credits that has endeared his students to him in recent years is the fact that Richard appeared at a Lincoln Center jazz event and was able to sing, play acoustic and electric bass, and play the pan, with an eclectic company of Caribbean-born, US-based musicians. This gig with high caliber musicians who specialize in Caribbean music was a major turning point in the journey to establish Richard as a musical communicator par excellence. Richard viewed this opportunity to play on a set with a group with international musicians as "an endorsement of the fact that at least I can be recognized as a pan player or make a contribution to the few pan players/soloists and be on stage with these wonderful musicians" as an equal with them.

Where the Rubber Meets the Road

There are many models that Richard holds up to his students and fellow musicians when he is rehearsing, performing, or teaching them the styles of music that come from his childhood resources. Apart from moving to the music that he plays with fellow musicians and students, he feels it is all right to do anything, "orthodox or unorthodox," to get them to play as if they were born and raised on the island where he came from. He wants his band of fellow musicians and jazz students to create the sound the way that he remembered his role models created it when he was learning the ropes of a professional musician in his native country. One of those heroes on the musical scene at the time of Richard's launch into the performance world was a young man who had studied in London, returned to his home, and began sharing his experiments with the Caribbean sounds he grew up hearing.

Richard said that he was "really impressed with the kind of work that [this returnee] was doing" as he fused Caribbean styles with Jazz standards. Also, Richard recalled that there was another musician on the scene who was blending classical Eastern music with the melodies that the island produced in the 1970s. This kind of fusion of local music traditions and North American influences made Richard "really excited" since he saw "himself" going in that direction before I could even define it." He knew back then that his journey would be shaped by his "wanting to experiment rather than just play calypso" so he could "get to some point where the music that I played and what I would be associated with came out of my experience with all this music in [my country]." Richard was also concerned that what he created and played as a professional showed "respect for the folks and the traditions, and certainly the Yoruba traditions [from Africa]" and other islands in the Caribbean.

Another musical idol who had tremendous influence on Richard is described more as a "tune smith" who created "simpler melodies, more procession driven as opposed to . . . driven by improvisation." This song writer was not known for being a "jazz artist [or] so much into improvisation," as the two former musicians mentioned in Richard's review of his music education on the island of his birth. However, his influence was deep enough on the country's musicians that Richard created a tribute in his honor and invited his original band members and one of his students from the jazz school to perform the work at a college in Connecticut. As with other programs Richard has created, directed, and played, he worked from the belief that "it's not music that they hear all the time" and he rehearsed in order to get the band "to sound as . . . refined as it possibly could."

The musical director knew that " . . . whatever you do on the top [of the music], whether you sing, have great vocalists . . . singing the lyrics, if you don't get that rhythm section happening . . . it's not going to be the same experience [as having traditional musicians from his home]."

What he achieved in this experience at the tribute performance with the musicians in his band was an example of what happens when, as with the drummer who was a student of Richard's at the time, players were "able to open up and embrace all these other styles that are so much part of the music today [in the USA]." Richard counted this show as another success on the road to making his island music accessible to a wider audience than the home fans who grew up listening to the sounds of the musicians who created work in their midst.

In another setting Richard worked with colleagues and students for the annual presentation of the styles of percussion that the International Jazz School promotes through classes and workshops. An assistant professor at the time, Richard was able to "arrive at that point where [the musicians] understand these nuances and strains from other types of music" by the time the show opened. Again, he achieved his goal by "singing things for them, you know, dancing and showing how the rhythms should make your body move [in order to] get them" on the same musical page. The journey to a high level of success was based on Richard deciding that he should choose "music that would be reflective [of] and paying respect to the composers that I would like to pay respect to [and] trying to find melodies that would be accessible to these musicians" who had a very short rehearsal time. Richard also planned his program based on the idea that " . . . [he] decided that the presentation needed to be about exposing the music of the couple of composers from [his home] whose music [he found by] looking through my recordings just to see what material I had from these composers that I hadn't done before."

Uppermost in Richard's mind was the fact that the music should "not be too challenging for the musicians" since he is always aware that he had to accommodate their level of comfort with relating to basic elements in the style of the music. The success of the set at the school demonstration was based on the fact that " . . . we are doing improvised music so if something happens on stage and you want this thing to go longer or it takes a detour that you didn't plan, that's okay as long as . . . the band members are really connecting then it's great, you just let it go."

In the ideal world of this Caribbean musician he would be a member of a performing group where "you have people who are [on] equal footing [as players] or who see themselves on equal footing, and working towards just getting better and better." By way of making his point about improving at a consistent pace over the course of a career, he mentioned the opportunity that jazz players in the USA created when bebop and swing were being perfected in clubs and concerts where musicians could polish their style of playing by being " . . . able to go and play and play three and four sets a night and then go and jam at each other's houses and so on and play and play and play and play and play the same shows over and over and over and over and make several recordings and play in each other's recordings." The result of this kind of performance culture among the musicians was that the high quality of the music still influences what we choose to buy and listen to fifty years after the recordings were made.

Musicians that played his compositions in the USA did not have that freedom to play as frequently as the predecessors that he mentioned in his review of the evolution of swing and bebop and other North American music traditions. On the other hand, when Richard talked about the pan players he respected and aspired to emulate, he admitted that very few of the musicians from his native land "figured out how to do [exceptional improvisation on the steelpan] without anybody teaching them and holding their hands." Besides the fact that these master players worked out of passion for the instrument and their ability to communicate their ideas in a particularly Caribbean voice, there were other cultural aspects that were working to make the artists function at a very high level. What he espoused as being at the heart of the excellence that he celebrates in these musicians and other artists of the theater that he grew up looking at and admiring is the fact that "the essence of what they did was using all the experiences . . . using the [traditional] mas[querade] and the carnival and the folk traditions: African and East Indian, and . . . the bongo [from Africa] . . . those threads [that] were all running through all the stuff" that they learned through living in their native land. The mastery of the pan instrument, therefore, was another effort "to portray the beauty, the culture of [their home in the Caribbean] and say so much about the people."

Of course, there are obstacles along the way to achieving these lofty musical goals. The multi-talented musician explained that the respect from "the Western" and particularly the people from his island in the northern-western state where he lives and works is not considerable. Further, in Richard's eyes, their respect or "their openness to embrace all the music" that comes out of the Caribbean leaves much to be desired. This exacerbates the situation where there is a small number of pannists who "really . . . seriously studied the art of improvisation as it applies to the [pan] and they don't have a lot of material" to work with. Filling this void of material is one of the pressing concerns that motivates Richard's many projects outside of teaching and playing professionally.

Providing transcripts of scores from the music of "master" composers to young musicians is an effort, in Richard's menu of interventions, that is guided by "the intention of helping young musicians connect with dedicating themselves to serious . . . really professional musician[ship] and seeing what kinds of skills are necessary." Richard is committed to young musicians who represent " . . . a [Caribbean] artist who is so rooted in [his island music] and who understands [the island] culture so much that they are trying to portray it in the best way that they can . . . that . . . people who have . . . a good sense of really fine art can appreciate [the level of mastery and artistic excellence]." As a master teacher himself Richard is informed by the vision which supports the ideal that the pannists can achieve musical excellence through study and practice on the instrument.

The Wind Beneath His Wings

Projects are the glue that keeps the teaching, writing, performing, and learning moving along on the tracks of Richard's dream of a more integrated lifestyle. He recalled several collaborations that made him feel like an accomplished musician. One of these ventures was a chance to record with a musician who won a Grammy award. The composer has "several CDs writing children's songs" and Richard was invited to record "a piece" with him. The composer just sent "a basic sketch of the tune" to Richard because he wanted a "steel drum player" to do the music. This work made Richard convinced that "this is a kind of thing that puts you in a different bracket, you know, people see your name and [you] get associated with somebody who's doing really good work." It is the ideal situation Richard continually strives to attain with his projects.

Another successful idea that came to fruition during one of Richard's teaching journeys involved faculty and students at International School of Jazz. The theme for the annual Black History Month celebration was chosen to present cross currents that blended Afro-Caribbean (drum scores) rhythms and songs so that students had a unified experience of music from the African Diaspora and did not get slots for separate musical items on the program. Richard described this effort as representative of "the position from which I work or try to create material . . . [since I am always] thinking of all these [cultural] influences" and want the students to experience the breadth of music that the Caribbean and Latin America represent. The music represented included Jamaican reggae, Afro-Cuban, and folk music and calypso from some of the islands in the Caribbean. Richard considered this production a success because the students "were able to see [the faculty] do a collaborative project and we tried to find ways that we [could] have the students overlap" in the music selections that were chosen for the show. The other important features of the February concert included the fact that "the community does come out to [see the show] so [the students] are required to at least step up to the plate" and "they certainly have to be a lot more professional and prepared" than they usually are when they just invite roommates and friends from the jazz school to their presentations.

One challenge of doing collaborative projects outside the International Jazz School campus is the dependence on sponsorship and volunteer labor to handle the administration of ticket sales and community outreach for the events. Richard invested a lot of energy and time in a community effort to bring three steelbands together in what he thought would result in a premier of several original scores by himself and other musicians. This was to be a chance for young people with Caribbean roots to learn some of the music that their parents grew up listening to and appreciate the heritage that the music represented. The leaders of the community wanted Richard to "write material . . . [and] bring people together who could play this music who are interested in doing it and performing it well."

In this community celebration of Caribbean heritage, which Richard thought was "a great idea" and a golden opportunity for him to connect with his "island people," he "offered to write a piece because . . . we were going to work with three steel bands in the community" in an effort to "bring them closer to . . . their cultural roots." The idea was to do a project that would work to counter the fact that the students "are so absorbed and enamored by the popular African American culture" as they are "hearing it every day and it's all around you and that's what they've been attracted to."

By the time the rehearsals began for the concert, however, "just one . . . band" was practicing "a nice mix of music and music that reflected not just [his native island] since other [Caribbean] islands were being reflected in the composition of the band and the community. The band learned "a couple of new pieces" and this was a result of Richard having to "sit and conceive ideas, work on them, discuss them." He also "went to see the theatre, talked to the sound person, talked about risers, how best we could [arrange] the space" and "all of the ground work to try to make it a good event." It was Richard's dream that the concert could be the test run for the show so that later on the organizers would find people to help "look for sponsors" and they "could think of taking the show on the road during the summer." Visits to other parts of the state and events out of state were part of the big scheme in Richard's mind. Unfortunately, a lack of ticket sales caused the organizers to cancel the concert. This fact further supported Richard's contention that Caribbean people in his town "don't really support Caribbean art and culture" even when someone is "trying to feature [their] own kids and trying to bring them closer to something . . . that we're losing" as the culture gets overwhelmed by North American idioms in dance and music.

Since Richard is always learning from his experiences, good or bad, he had to admit that "I wrote an original piece . . . [and it will] hopefully be played by somebody else. . . . Maybe I'll do it in my school, my college ensemble at some point." He also came to understand that the fault of the organizers lay in their inability to sell the concert to surrounding schools who would have taken an interest in the premier of the music that was created for the steelband. He analyzed the situation

and decided that the promoters of the concert could have gone to " . . .
elementary schools and offered them tickets at a reduced cost to come to
this concert and [they could have pointed out that the community players were in the band] performing and . . . even if they don't go to your
schools, it'd be great if you got kids from other schools of their own
age coming out to see them." The organizers could also have worked to
promote the orchestra in a "larger city . . . [and add] events at colleges,
schools" and other venues in later years.

Richard also worked on the community concert as an opportunity
for the young musicians to study writing by a composer with whom
they otherwise "wouldn't really have access to" since the steelbands
usually do covers of popular North American music that they hear on
the radio. The unfortunate part of playing this kind of music, Richard
admitted, is that the musicians are not "moving to the next level and
[learning] music written specifically for them or written for the instrument." The gift of Richard's involvement in the program was to be
understood as both the fact that he was trying to "get them to connect"
with their cultural roots, since he wants "to be involved more . . . with
the community," as well as having the young players exposed to a
composer "who understands the instrument . . . . how you want to see
the instrument displayed, promoted, reinterpreted."

Richard was initially excited by the idea that he would "be able to
write material that showcases really the breadth of the instrument. . . .
And also if you have really good players you could write stuff just like
any other ensemble that helps feature these players." Richard hoped
that this Caribbean community ensemble would do just as well as one
of the other steelbands that studied and played under his direction. He
wanted the community concert players to rise to the standard where
they could "play for the inauguration of Governor" and be significant
for being "a first" for that group and the community.

Creating CDs for the sake of his own plans for laying down a legacy
and giving a gift of the rich resources that have been untapped in the
melodies of his homeland music is another important project that takes
up time and focus in Richard's life. Richard wants to "be able to write
and [continue] . . . this little journey here of being able to take these
[Caribbean] composers and rework the material and write more material

that adds to the repertoire of the stuff that's out there" so that young musicians can study the work and later on add to the repertoire that Richard is building in Calypso Jazz music. He believes that this sustained effort of transcribing old melodies and reworking them to adapt current grooves could become a vital part of the national music festival that is held on his home island every year.

The transcriptions of the material that Richard has been doing is supposed to "help young improvisers" and he has "taken that material . . . transcribe[d] it for piano . . . arranging it . . . as a classical piece, [making sure that] all the technical stuff is still there." The paucity of scores that are now being used at this national competition, in Richard's estimation, is due partly to the lack of "the choice of the material." His contribution to the effort to train young musicians comes about when he needs to "arrange for band" and he is forced to write "some short arrangements."

When Richard arranges music for his recordings he has a "chance to put the music out how I hear it" and make it clear to the learned listener about "whoever else has influenced" his musical expression. The legacy of one of his earliest mentors is captured in the title of his first CD which was "about keepers of tradition" and his five original compositions were mixed with compositions that were "25–30 years old." He was certain when he began selecting pieces for the CD that some of the music was only recorded once, and so his mission was to "pull out these gems and give it a new treatment." Richard didn't "feel the need to be selfish" and to make the whole CD a showcase for his original music. He made sure to include music from "my people," the composers he played with soon after he left high school and became a professional musician. He didn't see any reason why he should be "paying royalties to Gershwin" or other non-Caribbean composers since he admitted that "I like the [Caribbean] music. It speaks to me," and it also stamps me as a man with a particular cultural history. He turned one calypso into a gospel rendition and the composer said "he didn't think of it that way" when it was first created and he was "really happy" about Richard's arrangement of the original melody.

The Man in the Mirror

Richard could be described as the "father figure" in the lives of his students. The fact that he feels strongly about his role in his students' lives as performers and developing artists comes across in the way that he retells stories about his experiences with his wards in and outside of the classroom. He feels most rewarded when he has been able to shape a student's compositional skills and contributed to his or her sense of being open and willing to learn from all avenues of art. Expressions in music, history, literature, painting, and dance are all part of the landscape from which Richard feels his students should be absorbing and learning to cull information and inspiration for their individual creations as artists. When he teaches music in his arranging class, he adds movement to the experience so that students get a kinesthetic appreciation of the idea that he is trying to impart through sound.

It would be easy for Richard to do the same kinds of exercises in his classroom every year since he has been at the International School of Jazz and teaching the same classes for over eight years. Yet he keeps looking for new recordings, new material in the repertoire he has collected, that would demonstrate the kind of feeling and technique that he wants his students to master. It is one of his ongoing projects to transcribe many of the melodies that he has collected from calypsonians and other musicians in his native country. Without this arsenal of material for his students to study from and learn to understand, Richard believes that they will continue to keep their superficial ideas about what Caribbean music is about and be left behind in the music evolution that is taking place in countries where the art form is continually being developed.

When students seek out Richard for individual lessons, or ask him to visit their gigs off campus, he takes it as a signal that a deep personal bond is being developed between him and the students in question. Asking for a master class, a book to read on a special topic that Richard introduced in a class, or a second opinion on a composition in their repertoire are all conversation starters in what turned out in several cases to be very satisfying relationships for students and teacher. Richard remembered one student who had a lot of difficulty composing songs in English and eventually decided to write music that was based on her childhood experiences in South America. Over time this student got a band of like-minded musicians together in the school and they performed on the streets in their town. The band went on to get a record deal and has established itself as a good performance group. Richard smiled when he recollected how this female struggled (with the diction and the arrangements in class) in the jazz arrangement class and in due course then found her unique way of communicating the music that she felt was representative of her home and its people.

Another student who was brought to mind when Richard talked about making connections with his young stewards was the drummer who made the cut when the Old Boys Jazz Festival in Richard's native island invited him to bring his group of musicians to perform on the show. Antoine was a well-respected drummer on campus at the time Richard was looking for someone to complete his quartet for the show on the island where he was born. He heard from other musicians, all part of the "little jazz scene" on campus, that Antoine was a talented and serious student. Previously, when Richard invited this young player to join him at a concert in honor of one of the island's most respected and successful songsmiths, Antoine was happy to join the cast that included faculty members. At that time, Richard was impressed by Antoine's "discipline" and recalled the seriousness with which he approached the task of learning the music for the memorial concert in Connecticut.

The young drummer recorded rehearsals and came back to every meeting with the full band ready to exhibit his confidence in the new material and to put his new skills into action and learn from the collective experience of playing Caribbean music with experienced elders. Not only did Antoine do very well at the concert where many natives of Richard's island were in attendance, including the wife of the musician who was being celebrated, but he made Richard very proud as a representative of the International Jazz School. Antoine paid attention to the musical information that the other musicians were feeding to him during the concert and he did not go for the choices of "playing a lot of notes" or "being loud" when he had his chance to show his stuff.

The very talent that Richard's old time friend Winston points out as necessary for success with Richard, as a student, is what Antoine represented to his classmates. The talent that a musician brings to the school setting has to be enhanced by "being prepared" and disciplined. According to his two oldest colleagues and band members, these are the qualities that a young student must present to the table in order to be successful with Richard. The other items on a bullet list of requirements that Winston, a player on Richard's first CD, included were good communication skills and a level of preparedness that show the student's capacity to take instruction and make use of it. Though Winston lamented the fact that Richard often has to teach students who are not ready for the intense conservatory experience that the International Jazz School professes to offer them, he still believed that Richard did a fine job with those students who were committed to learning and practicing the music recommended to them.

One pianist who graduated from the Jazz School's program has joined Richard's ensemble. This is a result of the musician's hard work and genuine interest in carving out his own voice from all the influences he was exposed to during his time at the school. Richard has been a mentor and is impressed by the studious approach that the pianist has taken in rehearsals. He writes down the new pieces that he learns in rehearsals, he practices the dances that Richard shows him for different scores, and he always comes back into the next session much more informed and confident about what he is presenting. Richard is aware that this young man is searching for an original way to express his voice on the piano, and he is happy to be one of the people to direct and inform the approach that he takes to building his repertoire as an Afro-American artist, Black male, North American citizen.

Ray, a fellow performer from back on the island, reflected on the fact that Richard has become so immersed in his teaching and improving the presentations that he does for his students that he has put off a lot of chances to perform. Richard, in his friend's understanding, sees his role as a musician, musicologist, historian, artist, and impresario as all one package that must be delivered with professionalism. When he "puts down his instrument" he must be able to talk about the history of the pan and the evolution of pan playing since the early 1960s. Richard is known for the fact that he has no respect for musicians who can only play their instrument and are left speechless when they need to answer a question from the audience about the history of the music that they play, or make a statement that will inform a student's appreciation of the genre of music that is being played in a demonstration or workshop.

As Richard described his passion for educating the uninitiated in his music tradition, he said: "I'd like to do more college and high school clinics—things which would allow me to refine my whole concept of this [genre of music] and a chance to play [for] the audience as well. I see myself doing more of this work over time." This pursuit of excellence in the arena of information on Caribbean music and culture has driven Richard to think hard about the kind of college presentations that he and a band of musicians can distribute across the country. The veteran teacher has begun to work on a video presentation and finding the right music that he could use in demonstrations in order to help listeners appreciate the music that he is committed to adding to the present jazz repertoire.

When there is a chance to present the pan as a percussion instrument to young students who are thinking about joining the International Jazz School, Richard recognizes it as a good place for musicians to " . . . see a [native musician] present the instrument, someone who [is knowledgeable] about the history . . . about the composers. . . . [who] they don't hear at all, and largely because the material is not available. . . . even if . . . CDs [are] available they don't get the airplay on the commercial stations."

Thoughts about the way that Richard would like to make a contribution to the young musicians from his home country concern the lack of material that is available to them for studying the work of their elders in the music world. He doesn't believe that a "young piano player," for example, has to go through the rites of passage of playing in the island's national pan competition for several years so that he can learn contemporary compositions from calypsonians. The pianist may not even be interested in learning music by Parker, Duke, or Monk in order to discern where he wants to put in his blend of music that combines Caribbean and North American heritages, so that he is even more severely hampered in the range of ideas that he can express through his compositions that are based on his island experience. Richard lamented that "the range of music things I recorded [on the island] they somehow get lost [over] a couple years, you can't find them except you go [visit] somebody's house and they're a collector." So the composer believes that it is a dire need "to be able to make information available" so that young pannists and other musicians can have local material that will inform their musical palette and expand their education.

Elegy for the 'Gour

Bronze medal, middle weight.
I want you to, I want you to you know
  that my father used pieces
    of old railway tracks to train.
into the gyms where White Trinidadians

And I want you to know that my
father told me,
and this is the first time I'm saying
this publicly,
if he pulls my toe tonight
I will call you tomorrow morning.

His experience
was

so deep
and was
so harsh
that he could
only
use that experience
to save
  that
  of experience
  for this book

Helsinki, 1952
I want you to know
that my father
wasn't allowed
were training in that
time.

My father told me,
do not come back
to Trinidad and Tobago.
I was banned from
returning
to Trinidad.

I'm so glad that you
  remembered him
  riding
his red motorcycle.
I had tears
in my eyes
when I read
that note from you.

me from having
kind
the reason
the season for thanks

Chapter Six

Cross-Case Analysis

"From the heart of life . . . the giants rise like winds, ascend like clouds, and, convene like mountains."

~Kahlil Gibran

The stories of these artists' lives in their professional tracks and the classrooms where they have trained students to join the ranks of others in the performing arts are filled with many similarities. The following discussion looks at the themes that evolve from the answers to each of the major questions that shaped the interviews at each of the three sessions with each artist. I also quote some of the colleagues and friends from the social network in order to fill out the picture that evolved from the responses to questions that were used as prompts in our discussions about the artists.

During the first interview with each artist the questions included: How did you come to be a professor at your institution? The intention was to find out as much as possible about the artist's life leading up to his present position in higher education, and to his status as a Black man with a career in the performing arts. In the quotes that are presented below the artists describe their interests in the various creative professions from their formative years.

Hugo, the dramatist:

> Maybe around 7 years old . . . a school teacher came and said I want . . . this child to take part in a play that I'm writing. She was a woman called Miss Childress. . . . And she was my primary school teacher at that point. . . . And so it was all the older students who were doing that play and there's a little role for a kid in it and when I went in to the rehearsals anything they asked me to do, I jumped up and did it. . . . And they continued re-writing and re-writing my part until I had just a big enough part, I was singing in it, I was dancing in it.

Gerard, the lighting designer:

> [It's been an] interesting sort of journey in that the interest was way back in high school, as a matter of fact. It is very funny because [another artist], God rest his soul, has had an influence on where I am today, I think. . . . [he] is the one, who said, "look, [Theater Works] is doing something . . . so let's go and see what is happening." I don't think I would have had that initiative on my own in those days. The rest is history because I developed a good relationship with [Theater Works].

Leo, the dancer/choreographer:

> Since I began to be . . . director of dance in [my native island] . . . I was nineteen years old, because I guess I was given such a role at such a young age, I never gave up the solidarity with dancers. . . . my solidarity was never with the people who were in charge of me. . . . I became even more close to the dancers, in terms of wanting the best for them, wanting to protect them, wanting to make sure that they got the best of everything.

In Richard's case, one of his musician colleagues and associates from the creation of the first CD produced by the composer remembered that they "grew up almost in the same generation of parents, who were very strict" and it meant that there were certain restrictions on their activities as young people.

Across the responses provided by the four artists, there was also a theme about the effort to move from amateur practitioner to professional craftsman. The major issue for these creative men was the transition from an island environment to a mainland, international sometimes, setting.

Richard, the composer, described his reason for going to music school:

> At some point, I think I realized I was getting older and I didn't want to be running around the world with a lot of musicians who were good musicians and I liked their abilities but when we took music apart, I found we really did not have much to discuss. For one, I was an older student. People were asking me how to do things and so on. . . . When we took the music apart, I was out of sorts. One, we were different culturally, I was older and . . . I already had a music career. . . . I didn't care to be staying in hotels and buses and so on.

Gerard, the lighting director/designer, who left his native country in his 20s explained his reasoning in these words:

> First to get my bachelor's degree at a [university]. And that was a nice little long story to get there . . . and then worked in New York for a bit. . . . Then I decided to go back and get my master's, which was a huge deal. . . . I eventually got it together and that was a big financial decision to become a student again. . . . I taught [at that university] as a teaching assistant while I was working on my master's and then graduated . . . [then] went back there as a lecturer for 3 years.

The next question during the first interview was about the details of a day in the life as an artist and teacher. The prompts such as "If you had to train an actor to portray you, what would be the menu that they would have to become familiar with?" were designed to find out about the kinds of activities that would fill the artist's daily round. The professors gave answers that detailed the intensity of their commitment to students and the hectic pace of the daily grind in school programs.

Leo, the dancer/choreographer:

> I just check my phones and I check my emails and do some quick correspondence or . . . see if there is anything I have to produce at the school that day, whether it's grades or . . . meetings or anything like that that I am responsible for, and then . . . I prepare myself, I do a little bit of meditation and . . . I have introduced my meditation to my students which they love and I have discovered that they are producing much better work with the meditation.

Richard, the musician/composer:

I want to stay home and write, but I have this responsibility and I have to show up and . . . the students know I will be there instead of them waiting, they know I am going to be there . . . I usually try to be prepared. . . . Even though I have been teaching the same classes for the past eight years, I am not one of those people who just kind of use the same material. I have to do this for my own sake just to try to find something in my collection, try to find some song, some jewel that will better exemplify something I am teaching, support the materials. . . . I am always looking for new material, revising stuff that I have done.

Gerard, the lighting designer/manager:

I want my own students to check in and [let me] see how they are progressing [on their projects]. So it is a very busy thing. That part of the package I think in education transcends what you teach and what you do professionally. It is all part of that process . . . you just have to go from one project to the next and in class we are doing [a] show. We have the spring show coming up and I have a lot of projects over the summer that I am already well into. It is always a juggle.

Finally, during my first interview, I asked each artist about his experience as a Black man with a career in the arts and education and what it meant to him. Further prompts like: "If we think about that journey as a chapter in your book called life, tell me what this chapter means . . . and where does it fit in the book that you have been living?" The main theme of learning and growing in the arts was reported across the answers from the artists/scholars. Some responses are below.

Gerard, the lighting designer:

It's always a little bit different when you work with a new [theater] group for the first time because you have to establish that kind of family relationship with them and then, you know, see where it goes from there. That's the kind of interesting part of this book, called a chapter, is the new connections that come along. . . . I find that to be something that is different because, yes, there's a million ways to do the Shakespeare . . . but [each artist] still brings a whole different ballgame to the design process because it's still going and still trying to find its way home.

Leo, the dancer:

What has been enjoyable [along the journey] is the learning process of learning how to make that living, how to have [the students] learn and that has been the greatest joy, when I see that. And many of them are now dancing in some of the major dance companies in the country . . . some of my students who I have mentored and coached at the [arts school in New York] and at the [American Modern Dance Company] that I danced in and I am making these recommendations for them and all that sort of stuff. That is a great joy.

Finally, there is the comment from Richard, the musician:

I have always done a lot of things, I have been in different institutions . . . and even though I am trying to cover a lot more disciplines . . . I am going to continue to have a lot of interests and be the best in this particular narrow topic [of calypso jazz]. . . . So I see the professor thing as just another hat. I can do this, I work hard and try to do it well, to the best of my ability and with confidence. . . . I needed to develop that part of me and it is something I can always come back on.

When I met with the artist scholars for the second interview, conducted a year after the first meeting, I was interested in finding out about "the highlights of the last year as a teacher and artist." My focus was on what had gone on in their classrooms and professional lives over the preceding year. I asked specifically about peaks and valleys of the teaching journey and productions.

Gerard, the lighting designer, boasted about his students:

[The student] was my assistant on that [production of *Jesus Christ, Superstar* in the Caribbean production], he has been hired by Global Staging along with his classmate of that year. They both are working there and doing well . . . doing things like Mary Kay Industrial, J-Lo Tour, ah . . . huge huge Rock 'n' Roll type things . . . R. Kelly, you name it . . . . they just sent me all their stuff today.

Gerard also lamented that he had to cut one of his graduate students from the lighting design program. As he described the situation:

At the end of this last academic year in May, I had two grads and one of them I needed to . . . cut him, it was not a good idea [for him] to continue in the program, for various reasons. Not that he wasn't talented but, this is the trouble when you have students leave school for too long and decide to come back, the pace in which they produce the work is not the pace we expect . . . it would take them maybe three times [as] long to come up with the design and when you're in tech[nology] you don't have three times as long, you have three times as short to be able to pull [the lighting design] off.

Richard, the musician, talked about the evolution of one of his students during the rehearsal and performance journey to a celebration concert in honor of one of the Caribbean's famous lyricists. Richard enthused:

He's young, he is coming up in a time where again, he's . . . certainly influenced by the whole contemporary jazz and hip-hop music. . . . And he's great at doing that, but I like the fact that he . . . sees himself being able to open up and embrace all these other styles [including Caribbean rhythms] that are so much part of the music today. So I like his attitude, he was easy to work with, so that's how I got him involved [in the concert].

Also, Leo had a few comments about his journey with the two female students who won prizes in the national competition for artistic advancement. Leo explained his process with choreographing for the winners this way:

I choreographed solos for [the two young women] . . . the solo for one girl was based on one that I did [for the annual dance concert at the high school program]. . . . And the other was based . . . on something that I was working on and that had to do with the goddess Oyo from the [Yoruba tradition], goddess of the wind and storms, and has dominion over . . . instances [of] death and the cemetery.

In the case of Hugo, the retired dramatist/dancer, his wife Felicia recalled his influence on students in this comment:

I would say that a big highlight in Hugo's career was his success as a teacher. Along the way he did have several successes as a director and a performer but . . . the biggest one was the teaching aspect and particularly the development of teaching movement to actors. He had a number of very successful productions that he worked with . . . but those sort of things are fleeting, they leave and they disappear—where as the teaching aspect remains because there are so many students that are still around who have been influenced by him and taught by him.

The final year interviews with the artist/scholars were designed to find out about what had taken place over one year in three cases, and with one artist we had to cover the events that happened over three years. Questions to the artists included (a) "What have been the highlights this year?"; (b) "Talk about your highlights as a teacher"; (c) "Tell me about . . . any students or any performance, any star moments where you as a teacher felt . . . it's coming together"; and (d) "Any other thoughts or feelings about this journey called being a professor in higher education?"

The theme that flowed through the answers to the prompts listed represented the productions that had been accomplished over the time that the artists had been working at their individual schools and the various professional outlets with which they are associated. Following are some of the comments that the artists shared about their creative productions.

Richard, the musician, explained:

> After [the score] was performed the first time, I said you know something . . . I'll just rename this tune for my sister and then, you know, she's celebrating . . . her 50th birthday, so . . . it was good to have to write that. I just wrote a tune and it's going to be . . . whenever the next CD gets done, it's going to be on there. . . . This was written in a somber style and I know that she particularly likes [songs] but I don't know why I made that connection. . . . That's what came to me.

Gerard, the lighting designer who was out of touch with me for three years, told me about his successes. These products included the creation of the first lighting design program at a new university on his home island. Gerard told me:

> [At one stage of the process] we had to go back to square one and re-write the substantial documents [describing the program] and that took several months to finish, and then that went . . . to the validation committee and then it went through that process, and it went to the Academic Council, which is you know, professors at the university. And it passed that hurdle and then it was about to go to . . . be signed off by the Board of Governors, and then there was this [national] election and there was a big change in the government.

Leo, the dancer, had a lot to say about his students and their accomplishments during the international tour to South America that he was invited to direct. He described with great pride that:

> The great part of the tour is the fact that three of my students of [my dance program at the college] . . . [two of the students began studying with me] in high school and [continued in the program for] college and [the third student] I met in college, [who] are on the tour. . . . So it was great.

The choreographer continued to celebrate his students' progress as he relived their excitement during the residence of a major contemporary dance company at the college where he teaches. The artist explained:

> To be able to have my students realize the connection between the craftsman work that we do in daily technique classes and how that transfers itself into performance and to have professional dancers [demonstrate that fact] . . . [dancers] that are older, come in and do a lecture demonstration, teach technique classes, and then do a performance of their own. It helps [students] a lot to actually see other people do what [they] are doing [in their training program].

Hugo, the retired drama professor, talked about the book that he had begun and the exciting process of traveling across the world to meet people who helped him flesh out his research topic on the traditional folk performing arts of his native country. His former student, Bernard, described the professor's work in these words:

> [Hugo] is pursuing and interviewing a lot of the original players of traditional [folk characters] . . . who are still alive. The nature of the characters such as The Dragon, the King Sailor, etc., are now high priorities on his radar screen. . . . I have been extremely fortunate to read some of the written work he has completed and sent to me via email. They made me realize that his approach to this research project is not to simply rehearse sophistic descriptions of the theatrical processes within a pedagogical framework just for the benefit of Western taste publics. Prof is walking the "memory walk" with these original practitioners, who like him, understood and were spiritually attuned to the schemes of revolution employed since the dawn of civilization in the Nile Valley.

The Second Wave

Black notes make music
on a plain white sheet.
Black words make stories
that we can speak out loud

~Dinah Johnson

Other themes have been culled to describe the ways in which the stories from these 23 interviews from the artists and their network intersect and cross-reference each other. Topics on character, the philosophy that guides the artists/scholars in their professional lives, their working guidelines for training students, and the lasting impact that they have created among some of the graduates from their educational programs, are among the labels that can be used to describe this community of teachers and artist mentors.

Character Traits

Among the comments that members of the social networks shared about their colleagues/friend, were those remarks that described some aspect of their personality that caused the artist to stand out in the network members' minds.

In the case of Leo, his former teacher, Wendy, shared the following sentiments:

> I like to cook. You know, so we share all of those things and we are very comfortable [in each other's company]. And if there's an opinion I want or something, I don't hesitate to ask him. You know, to just run it by him. He may not have all of the answers but he is willing to listen and vice versa.

Gerard's network, in the dance department at Southern University, had a similar response to his level of hospitality and warmth in the company of students, friends, and colleagues. His collaborator, Nikki, at the university enthused when she explained:

> At this point, I think he's in the chapter [of my life] where I talk about people that I've met and I wish I could see them more often and be around them more

often. He's in that chapter, he's someone that I always [know] where I can find him, I will always know where he is, but I wish I could holler down the hall and say "hey, come in here." You know, he's in that chapter. I really miss him.

Guiding Philosophy

Several comments represent the moral and emotional parameters that inform the choices of these four artist/scholars. Feelings that were expressed by former students, teachers, performing artists from companies where they worked as members, or friends who had stayed on the artist's journey over several decades allow the observer to cull a perception of the esteem in which each professor is held by the commentator.

Bernard, who was a former student of Hugo, had this to say about the drama professor while he was the chair of the drama department before retiring to write his book and travel across the world. Bernard, now a movement specialist, was passionate while he described this perspective held by Hugo. On the issue of navigating a predominantly White academic and performing environment, the angle of engagement looked like:

> If you earned [Hugo's] respect, he would "elevate" you to share one of the many tales about his narrow escape from becoming just another exotic trophy on a hunter's wall while he journeyed towards his highest potential, and you would be amused, but not surprised that (like the typical African lion) he was able to get a "free meal" during the escape process.

When talking about his experiences with Richard, the musician, his former band member and longtime friend from his home island shared some insights about how Richard came to be respected in his field as a composer and musician. Gerard explained:

> If you approach him, work with him, he will give you the time [of day]. [Other musicians] say that he is very nice, he is musical, he plays, and he always tries to present what he is doing the best way possible. I know one thing about Richard . . . he is very much concerned about presentation. When he comes through the door, he will be on time, dressed well, present [him]self well, and the product will [sell] itself, and I totally agree with that. A lot of musicians

have problems with that . . . I think most musicians can learn a lot from him in terms of their presentation of their own group as well.

Mentoring

A prevailing perspective that stitches the comments of associates in the social networks of these scholars and teachers is the attitude that informs the journey that they take on with their students. Each artist spoke with pride about the long term relationships that they have sustained, and been nourished by, with regard to their students and apprentices.

Leo, the choreographer, remembers the trust that he established with his students when he created an environment for his new dancers to excel in his annual college dance concert. In one description of a student's journey to the final performance, Leo shared this insight:

> [Building trust] it's [like] feeding them, it's nursing them. You give them a little bit at a time that they can handle and as they start to get comfortable with it I go deeper, I bring more of the . . . dark information about the experiences that Nijinsky had. . . . So, they are not overwhelmed at the beginning and run away from it, or give up, but you give them a little taste and they can handle it and by the middle, then they go on and . . . slowly, but surely, you will not have to give them more [than] they ask for.

Janet, the production company director on Gerard's home island, talked about the design students who made a trip to her home island away from the North American college campus where Gerard was training the young lighting designers. Her words glowed with pride about the way that the young American men blended into the new cultural milieu that they had to contend with after arriving on the island to begin work on a technical crew. The veteran theater practitioner laid out her appraisal of the graduate students in these terms:

> Last year I met Jay. . . . Gerard brings the [graduate students] on board to assist him [in the professional stage productions] as he goes along. Jay seems to be self-confident and I know that he has gone on to do [work with other] projects . . . gone on to do quite amazing things. This year [Professor Gerard] brought

Ray. Ray was amazing as well, because Ray really jumped in. He was a butterfly, he was . . . really active in . . . expediting [the lighting plot]. Sometimes operators are a little laid back . . . so I know that particularly soon this year Ray was running [at the same pace as Gerard] . . . to make sure that's what he wanted [the show to look like].

Making a Lasting Impression

Each of the four artists has special memories of students or productions that touched them in a deep sense. The student was either exceptional in the level of growth that they demonstrated over a period of time, or the production on campus or off campus brought about a heightened level of performance excellence for all the participants. Here are some quotes from the interviews that were culled to reflect these experiences across all the artists' stories.

Richard, the composer, explained:

Seeing the influence you have on a young student, particularly someone coming in, green, bright-eyed and bushy-tailed, and then seeing them become players afterwards. You see the evidence of your instruction on your class and how you are able to reach them. You [say to yourself] . . . okay, this is something I can do. I can say I know a lot of students like that . . . some of them will actually come back and say thanks for talking to me about this . . . when I was in your class . . . those are the kinds of things that you want to hear as a reward. That is very rewarding.

Leo, the dancer, was moved to share his sense of gratitude for his dancers:

So the students were very moved, very inspired [by the visiting dance company from New York], they learned a lot and [were] able to realize that a lot of what I've been saying and working with them on, a lot that it actually works [for the students] to actually see it happen with another dance company because usually they don't see it for real [in the school]. Sometimes they'll need in their beginning stages as students to see other [professional] people do it and that was a big highlight, as well, as a teacher. Also, working with the dancers, these young dancers, on a piece like Nijinsky that requires so much breadth in terms of the use of the imagination and character building, to see them go from just learning steps, and movement, and owning the world and bringing themselves into the characters that they have to play and to see them grow and become confident.

Hugo, the dramatist, enthused when he described one student's decision to follow his advice about casting a show with an all-White group of theater students. He described his approach to the graduate student director in these words:

> These girls know [how to follow stage directions]. Find a common ground. They're all women. Abusive women is not a black phenomenon, you know, they must have aunts and mothers and sisters who have had bad relationships, or they themselves [have had such incidents] with their boyfriends. So what you [as the director] have to do is sit together in a circle of women and plug into that part of it and you're home free. All the other things of the blackness and things of that, you [don't] worry about that with them. Let them apply the [essence of the story] to their experiences. But of course, she decided to do it and to take my [advice] because she had one or two friends, black friends, who figured she'd sell out but she said, no, no my advisor professor Henry told me to do it. . . . He's the one who [told] me to do it this way . . . she did it. It was . . . successful in the department and in the theatre community.

Discussion

> "Like the human heart and its arteries, the imagination and intellect are inextricably linked; they develop simultaneously, and, I suggest, one is not possible without the other."
>
> ~Mary Weems (1990, p. 1)

Weems suggested that the lack of focus on the imagination-intellect has contributed to the undoing of public education. She proposed, in her ideal vision of a public school, five guidelines to help educators develop the kinds of schools where dreams are not deferred but supported and nourished. I discuss the 23 interviews and themes that I culled from the artists/scholars and their network of friends and colleagues within the framework that is proposed by Weems in her description of "Utopia" (p. 4). These tenets for an ideal school include (a) aesthetic appreciation, (b) oral expression, (c) written expression, (d) performance, and (e) social consciousness.

Aesthetic appreciation. Students who are exposed to a wide range of artistic expressions develop this point of view. The apprentices are led in discussions by trained teachers that help them develop an aesthetic sensibility and a critical eye that improves their appreciation of artistic creation as a part of human experience. In the descriptions of their creative processes with students the four artistes offer insights into the way that they support the individuality of a student's creative expression.

Leo, dancer/choreographer, said of his experiment with student voices in the creation of a new dance piece about the famous ballet dancer, Nijinsky:

> Working with . . . these young dancers on a piece like "*Nijinsky*" that requires so much breadth in terms of the use of the imagination and character building . . . young artists have to understand the craft to practice in it, to going through the rehearsal again and again and again, and coming to respect the craft and then bringing that language back to the classroom and seeing them become much more attentive in the classroom and more attentive and caring about the technique . . . and then bringing that back again into rehearsal. . . . That for me is the biggest highlight for me as a teacher for the year.

Gerard, the lighting designer, also commented on his support of the individual student's artistic vision and honing of the skills that make it possible to express that world view. The veteran designer explained:

> What you try to engender as an educator is to pull out that artist from the student, get them to expand their ideas on things, and some [schools promote a system where] everybody comes up with a scheme that looks the same. I'm not interested in that at all, so I look for two students every other year so that you can give them your full attention span for the three years that they're around [in the degree program].

Oral expression. The development of the improvised response to some prompt assists students in facing the fear of standing in front of an audience and presenting themselves in a manner that is complementary to their developing self-esteem. Similarly, the performing artist takes a cue from some aspect of the art that is being developed as a musician, dancer, lighting designer, or dramatist, and puts himself or herself in a position to express his or her innermost thoughts and feelings in a tangible way. The symbol system that is chosen for the communication of such ideas to an audience is informed by the artistic discipline in which the student creator is molded. Following are examples of the ways in which these artists under discussion have expressed their emotional and intellectual responses to a cue or symbol system in front of an audience.

Bernard, one of Hugo's former students, talked about his professor and the presentation that he made at an international conference for movement specialists. The professor explained:

> The [professional] practitioners and I looked on with delight while Hugo skillfully demonstrated his technique as a "King Sailor" dancer with "educated feet." As he danced and managed his space, we instinctively knew that what this gentleman understood about the [folk performing] traditional . . . characters, and his execution of this knowledge, firmly reinforced the durability of specific Caribbeanist aesthetics, or what many would describe as "the flash of the spirit" in [the folk tradition], where one relies on individual invention in the moment.

Richard, the musician, is known for his compositions. In a comment about a track on his first CD, Winston made this comment about the way in which Richard showed his personality through the performance on one of the tracks:

> I was very, very impressed with that particular [musical] arrangement. The treatment of the melody and the genre, in which he did it, to me, brought out a side of Richard that I was not aware of. . . . The level of musicality; you interact with musicians and then sometimes all of a sudden, there is something that pops up . . . people may not really be expecting [from you] and, you know . . . I think I have to say this, the reaction from that is, I didn't know that Richard was capable of that level of musicality. That really highlighted something that I didn't know about him.

Written expression. The effort to support students in their creation of products based on language and to learn how to respond to ideas that are represented in print communication is part of the artist's journey.

Excerpts from the scholars about their creative process help to illuminate this ideal of communicating effectively with the printed word.

Leo, the dancer/choreographer, talked about his students and their poetry writing:

> [I asked the students to] write some poetry or stories, [about] some experience in their life that was very important to them, that was very intense, perhaps traumatic whatever it was, that it meant a lot to them. . . . So they all wrote stories and brought it in [to rehearsal] . . . some of it was extremely tragic and violent, I mean just really emotional stuff. . . . So what I did was take some of that material and I took the ones that I felt that would be choreographical, if that's a word. You know, that which I felt . . . could bring a lot of movement to the theatre, a lot of . . . theatrical dynamic.

Gerard, the lighting designer, talked about the students using pencil or computer software to create their lighting plots. As an alternate form of written communication, his students learn to express their ideas to an audience in the theatre using the symbols that they have seen manipulated by lighting designers. Gerard explained:

> [The student designer has to] . . . go back to the director [of the play] and say this is what I'm thinking, is this what you can afford? What do you think of this movement and this movement? So very much like television, a story board, a series of images or photographs [is developed]. Some of these are hand sketches, some of them are using electronic visualization through different computer programs. Whatever technique they want to use it is quite fine by me, but you have to develop some visual image to show the directors and give the costume designers their sketches, so you can give examples, and models. . . . So lighting designers have to come up with the same kind of visual image.

Richard, the composer, talked about his support of student writing for the music composition program:

> Students can arrange an existing piece or compose something, or arrange . . . one of their own compositions. So we did a concert this past March and that was a good experience. . . . You have the students shape the pieces. . . . They might be too short, they may need to add something. They need to change the instrumentation a little bit. Things like that, and we work with them over a couple . . . of months. We have about . . . a month in which we do the rehearsal

. . . we work with them in terms of shaping . . . the piece, and I saw some . . . students who really shined through that process.

Performance. The focus on effective communication through rehearsed and memorized performances of published work demands an intense level of commitment on the part of the artist and apprentice in his care. Several descriptions of student presentations for the artists/scholars impressed the teachers and helped to flesh out the perception of quality achievements.

Hugo, the dramatist, directed *Waiting for Godot* with a Black and White cast in one of his theaters in Canada. One of his former cast members and students, Gerard, recalled the experience as an actor in that show. He shared this insight:

> One of the main highlights [of my career], was the production of *Waiting for Godot*. [Hugo] tackled that play here in [Canada]. It, as far as I can tell, until that time, was always done with a white cast and he mixed the casting, he had both African and Caucasian actors in that [show], which provided some dimensions to the production. . . . I had the opportunity, well I should say, he cast me in the role of Coco, which was quite a stretch for me because prior to that the only [acting I had done was in drama] school but having the opportunity to do a professional production of *Waiting for Godot* was certainly a highlight in my acting career.

Leo, the dancer, recalled the performance by one of his students in the annual high school concert. He reminisced:

> To come in with just . . . 14 months [of training], of just beginning to dance, he's a freshman, he's just for the first time learning the [Modern Dance] Technique and learning how to transfer dramatic information into dance movement, and to do it so quickly and so clearly and so vibrant[ly] and with so much passion, speaks to the naturalness of intelligence . . . that's accessible to every single human being on the planet. If one has a desire, as he does, and a will to express that intelligence in . . . any way you want, whether it's [as] a painter, an actor, a singer, a musician, a car builder, an inventor, any kind, it can happen if you have deep desire and will.

Social consciousness. Facets of history, diversity, social justice, and participatory democratic ideals are the focus of this feature of Weems's

Utopia. By engaging students in a world that looks through the lens that is created by feelings, facts, and intellectual curiosity, the four artists in this study promote a learning environment that facilitates the development of all the senses of their students. Excerpts from some of the stories about the ways in which students have experienced the impact of social issues as practitioners of their art in each field of dance, music, lighting design, and drama, allow the reader to look into the world of the productions that have been brought to life by these young apprentices.

Leo, the dancer/choreographer, enthused:

> The third section [of the dance suite] had the homeless woman walking through a group of women who were laughing at her as she fell. As she walked forward trying to move into a new space . . . I thought of [representing] the glass ceiling, you know, that even though they may be moving along and moving forward there's still a glass ceiling [that women have to contend with]. But also . . . the whole gender thing [since] those women can find a lot of opposition from women themselves. . . . As they try to move up, some of the most aggressive "beat down" will come from women themselves . . . and there is stiff competition [among the women] . . . or there are those who feel that you're going too far, or . . . there are those that might feel also . . . that there [are] some traditional aspects of womanhood that should remain intact . . . there are those who feel the workplace is no place for a traditional woman to just move forward.

In the case of Gerard's experience, he encourages students to read widely and to travel so that they can bring their experiences as well-exposed designers to bear on the elements that they create for the theater. He emphasized his perspective in this quote:

> [The designer's] mind is continuously active, you're rethinking, re-evaluating, and then coming up with an ever evolving ethic in that you have to keep constantly aware of what is going on in the world because . . . you're not just involved in theatre . . . it's a reflection of what's happening in the world. So, you have to be aware of what is going on in the world. You have to constantly do research. You have to read a lot. . . . How does that [international event] impact what you do? As any artist, it's what's happening around you that's going to affect the way you work, affect the way you see things, affect the way you produce things.

Conclusion

As we build learning contexts in which students and teachers enact a continual loop of communication that is supported by multiple forms of communication (Harste, 1994), or enact educational spaces where we answer Kist's (2010) question about the way we need to incorporate the study and production of texts in multiple media on a daily basis, we find it necessary to look for teachers who have transformed their classrooms in an effort to broaden the literacy of their students. We seek out places where we may find inspiration so that we can appreciate student productions that included forms such as dance, music, video production, sculpture, or music. The work that goes on in spaces where apprentice artists are being formed in the crucible of discipline, high standards, and the guiding precepts of the imagination-intellect in practice, gives teachers of all backgrounds the encouragement to do good by our highly communicative students. A quest for the models that will help us carve out dreams from our imagination and render us free to be brave in the face of our longing for ideal learning exchanges can bring us to classrooms like the ones that Hugo, Richard, Gerard, and Leo have described in their stories.

If imagination, as Sherman Alexie (1993) suggested, is the "politics of dreams" (pp. 152–153), then we have every right to claim our classrooms as that landscape where we enact beautiful dreams. Classrooms are sites where such becoming is possible and necessary. That precious space and time in which we hold students in our care, apprentices who will govern our world when we may not care to see, feel, or act in a global village that we helped to create, demand that we bring the visions of successful communication into reality. We, as teachers who believe in the arts as an exploration of our full humanness, can create a poem of interconnectedness with our students that resembles the creation that Kahlil Gibran (1960) described as "a sacred incarnation of a smile. . . . a sigh that dries the tears . . . a spirit who dwells in the soul, whose nourishment is the heart, whose wine is affection" (p. 8).

More specifically, we can encourage our students to engage with our experiences as learned elders in the spirit that Richard, the composer, has articulated through his teaching:

When I think of a student shining is when you make suggestions of how you can improve the piece, but you are sort of doing that with . . . your musical director hat on and then it works when it comes together, when it's performed. It works. It gets a good response. People enjoy it . . . because things fall into place. [The students] feel confident, because they start hearing, you know, they start seeing some of those suggestions that you made . . . it works eventually. As a student you may not know all those . . . answers. You need people to guide you and when you take that guidance, when you listen to a professional ear . . . when it works . . . you feel good about that . . . [so that] when they have to do it again they say okay, okay, you know what? I've learned something from these experiences or these stages [that I learned from my professors].

References

Alexie, S. (1993). *The Lone Ranger and Tonto fistfight in heaven*. New York: Harper Collins.

Barone, D. (2004). Case-study research. In N. K. Duke & M. H. Mallette (Eds.), *Literacy research methodologies* (pp. 7–27). New York, NY: The Guilford Press.

Beach, R., & Myers, J. (2001). Hypermedia authoring as critical literacy. *Journal of Adolescent & Adult Literacy, 44*, 538–46.

Bryce-Laporte, R. S. (1972). Black immigrants: The experience of invisibility and inequality. *Journal of Black Studies, 3*, 29–56.

Deaux, K. (2006). *To be an immigrant*. New York, NY: Sage.

Delpit, L., & Dowdy, J. K. (Eds.). (2002). *The skin that we speak: Thoughts on language and culture in the classroom*. New York, NY: The New Press.

Dodd, C. (1992). *Dynamics of intercultural communication*. Dubuque, IA: Wm. C. Brown.

Doig, L., & Sargent, J. (1996). Lights, camera, action. *Social Studies Review, 34*(3), 6–11.

Dowdy, J. K. (2009). *In the public eye*. Boardman, OH: Commess University.

Dowdy, J. (2008). Fire and ice: The wisdom of black women in the academy. New Horizons in Adult Education & Human Resource Development, *22*(1), 24–43. Retrieved from http://education.fiu.edu/newhorizons/journals/New%20Horizons%20in%20AEHRD%2022(1)%20Issue.pdf

Dowdy, J. K. (2008). *Ph.D. stories: Conversations with my sisters*. Creskill, NJ: Hampton Press.

Dowdy, J. K. (Ed.). (2005). *Readers of the quilt: Essays on being Black, female and literate.* Creskill, NJ: Hampton Press.

Dowdy, J. K. (2003). *GED stories: Black women and their struggle for social equity.* New York, NY: Peter Lang.

Dowdy, J. K., & Golden, S. (Eds.). (2011). *Connecting the literacy puzzle: Linking the professional, personal, and social literacies.* Creskill, NJ: Hampton Press.

Dowdy, J. K., & Wynne, J. (Eds.). (2005). *Racism, research, and educational reform: Voices from the city.* New York, NY: Peter Lang.

Gibran, K. (1960). *Thoughts and meditations.* Translated and Edited by A. R. Ferris. New York: The Citadel Press.

Glazer, N., & Moynihan, D. P. (1964). *Beyond the melting pot.* Cambridge, MA: MIT. Press and Harvard University Press.

Halliday, M. (1985). *An introduction to functional grammar.* London, England: Edward Arnold.

Harste, J. (1994). Visions of literacy. *Indiana Media Journal, 17*(1), 27–32.

Jacobs, D. (2007). More than words: Comics as a means of teaching multiple literacies. *English Journal, 96*(3), 19–25.

Kist, W. (2004). *New literacies in action: Teaching and learning in multiple media.* New York: Teachers College Press.

Jewitt, C., Kress, G., Ogborn, J., & Tsatsarelis, C. (2001). Exploring learning through visual, actional and linguistic communication: The multimodal environment of a science classroom. *Educational Review, 53,* 5–13.

Jones, T. (1990). Perspectives on ethnicity. In L. V. Moore (Ed.), *Evolving theoretical perspectives on students* (pp. 59–72). San Francisco, CA: Jossey-Bass.

Kalmijn, M. (1996). The socioeconomic assimilation of Caribbean American Blacks. *Social Forces, 74,* 911–930.

Kasinitz, P. (1992). *Caribbean New York: Black immigrants and the politics of race.* Ithaca, NY: Cornell University Press.

Keane, F., Tappen, R. M., Williams, C. L., & Rosselli, M. (2009). Comparison of African American and Afro-Caribbean older adults' self-reported health status, function, and substance use. *Journal of Black Psychology, 35,* 44–62.

Kist, W. (2002). Finding "new literacy" in action: An interdisciplinary high school Western civilization class. *Journal of Adolescent & Adult Literacy, 45,* 368–377.

Kress, G., & Van Leeuwen, T. (1996). *Reading images: The grammar of visual design.* London, England: Routledge.

Kress, G., Jewitt, C., Ogborn, J., & Tsatsarelis, C. (2001). *Multimodal teaching and learning: Rhetorics of the science classroom.* London, England: Continuum.

Lincoln, Y. S., & Guba, E. G. (1985). *Naturalistic inquiry.* Beverly Hills, CA: Sage.

Martinec, R. (1996). *Rhythm in multimodal texts.* London, England: The London Institute.

Merriam, S. (1988). *Case-study research in education: A qualitative approach.* San Francisco, CA: Jossey-Bass.

Model, S. (1991). Caribbean immigrants: A Black success story? *International Migration Review, 25,* 248–276.

O'Toole, M. (1994). *The language of displayed art.* Leicester, England: Leicester University Press.

Patterson, R. (2001). 26 ways of looking at a Black man: And other poems. In *Ashley Bryan's ABC of African American poetry.* New York, NY: Aladdin Paperbacks.

Patton, M. Q. (1990). *Qualitative evaluation and research methods* (2nd ed.). Newbury Park, CA: Sage.

Porter, R., & Samovar, L. (1994). An introduction to intercultural communication. In L. Samovar & R. Porter (Eds.), *Intercultural communication: A reader* (7th ed., pp. 4–26). Belmont, CA: Wadsworth.

Read, J. G., Emerson, M. O., & Tarlov, A. (2005). Implications of Black immigrant health for US racial disparities in health. *Journal of Immigrant Health. 7,* 205–212.

Reiff, J. C. (1992). *Learning styles: What research says to the teacher.* Washington, DC: National Education Association.

Rosenblatt, L. (1978). *The reader, the text, the poem: The transactional theory of the literary work.* Carbondale, Southern Illinois University Press.

Samovar, L., & Porter, R (1999). *Intercultural communication: A reader.* Belmont, CA: Wadsworth.

Samovar, L., Porter, R., & Jain, N. (1981). *Understanding intercultural communication.* Belmont, CA: Wadsworth.

Seidman, I. E. (1991*). Interviewing as qualitative research.* New York, NY: Teachers College Press.

Senge, P., Kleiner, A., Roberts, C., Ross, R., & Smith, B. (1994). Strategies for building shared vision. In P. M. Senge, A. Kleiner, C. Roberts, R. B. Ross, & B. J. Smith (Eds.), *The fifth discipline fieldbook: Strategies and tools for building a learning organization* (pp. 297–303). New York, NY: Doubleday.

Soeder, J. (2011, March 6). Grammy-winning jazz sensation Esperanza Spalding seeks to communicate at the highest levels through music. *The Plain Dealer.* Retrieved from http://www.cleveland.com/popmusic/index.ssf/2011/03/grammy_winner_esperanza_spaldi.html

Sowell, T. (1978). Three Black histories. In T. Sowell & L. D. Collins (Eds.), *Essays and data on American ethnic groups* (pp. 7–64). Washington, DC: The Urban Institute.

Stake, R. (2000). Case studies. In N. Denzin & Y. Lincoln (Eds.), *Handbook of qualitative research* (2nd ed., pp. 435–454). Thousand Oaks, CA: Sage.

Stephan, W., & Stephan, C. (1996). *Intergroup relations.* Boulder, CO: Westview Press.

Stewart, E., & Bennett, M. (1972). *American cultural patterns: A cross-cultural perspective.* Yarmouth, ME: Intercultural Press.

Strauss, A., & Corbin, J. (1990). *Basics of qualitative research: Grounded theory procedures and techniques.* Newbury Park, CA: Sage.

Tatum, B. (1997). The complexity of identity. *Why are all the Black kids sitting together in the cafeteria?* New York, NY: Basic Books.

Van Leeuwen, T. (1999). *Speech, music, sound.* London, England: Macmillan.

Walcott, D. The sea is history. Retrieved from http://www.poemhunter.com/poem/the-sea-is-history/

Waters, M. (1991). The role of lineage in identity formation among Black Americans. *Qualitative Sociology, 14,* 57–76.

Watkins-Owens, I. (1996). *Blood relations: Caribbean immigrants and the Harlem community, 1900–1930.* Bloomington, Indiana University Press.

Weems, M. E. (2003). *Public education and the imagination-intellect: I speak from the wound in my mouth.* New York, NY: Peter Lang.

Yin, R. (1994). *Case-study research: Design and methods* (2nd ed.). Thousand Oaks, CA: Sage.

Index

ROCHELLE BROCK &
RICHARD GREGGORY JOHNSON III,
Executive Editors

Black Studies and Critical Thinking is an interdisciplinary series which examines the intellectual traditions of and cultural contributions made by people of African descent throughout the world. Whether it is in literature, art, music, science, or academics, these contributions are vast and far-reaching. As we work to stretch the boundaries of knowledge and understanding of issues critical to the Black experience, this series offers a unique opportunity to study the social, economic, and political forces that have shaped the historic experience of Black America, and that continue to determine our future. Black Studies and Critical Thinking is positioned at the forefront of research on the Black experience, and is the source for dynamic, innovative, and creative exploration of the most vital issues facing African Americans. The series invites contributions from all disciplines but is specially suited for cultural studies, anthropology, history, sociology, literature, art, and music.

Subjects of interest include (but are not limited to):

- EDUCATION
- SOCIOLOGY
- HISTORY
- MEDIA/COMMUNICATION
- RELIGION/THEOLOGY
- WOMEN'S STUDIES

- POLICY STUDIES
- ADVERTISING
- AFRICAN AMERICAN STUDIES
- POLITICAL SCIENCE
- LGBT STUDIES

For additional information about this series or for the submission of manuscripts, please contact Dr. Brock (Indiana University Northwest) at brock2@iun.edu or Dr. Johnson (University of San Francisco) at rgjohnsoniii@usfca.edu.

To order other books in this series, please contact our Customer Service Department:

(800) 770-LANG (within the U.S.)
(212) 647-7706 (outside the U.S.)
(212) 647-7707 FAX

Or browse online by series at www.peterlang.com.